THE FINANCIAL BLUEPRINT

for Real Estate Agents

THE FINANCIAL BLUEPRINT for Real Estate Agents

Unveiling how top-producing agents keep more of their hard-earned money

Mike Ross and Nathan Ganz

NW PREMIER
PUBLISHING

The Financial Blueprint for Real Estate Agents
Unveiling how top-producing agents keep more of their hard-earned money

ISBN-13:
979-8-9895280-0-4 Paperback
979-8-9895280-1-1 Hardcover
979-8-9895280-2-8 eBook
LCCN: 2023921352
NW Premier Publishing
Vancouver, Washington

Disclaimer: The information provided in this book is for informational and educational purposes only and is substantially based on the opinions and experience of the owners of NW Premier, Nathan Ganz and Mike Ross. Neither Nathan Ganz nor Mike Ross are accountants, CPA's, bookkeepers, or attorneys. The information provided in this book is not intended in any way to be financial, accounting, or legal advice for you, the reader, to rely on. In all instances, the reader is encouraged to do their own independent research and to discuss the information provided in this book with their professional financial advisor, insurance broker, attorney, bookkeeper, or accountant. NW Premier, Nathan Ganz, and Mike Ross make no representations or warranties, express or implied, about the completeness, accuracy, reliability, or suitability of the information provided in this book for you or your business.

Endorsement

Having spent years in the real estate industry, I can confidently say that 'The Financial Blueprint for Real Estate Agents' is a game-changer. The authors Nathan, Mike, and their team are the real deal - their insights and strategies are practical, actionable, and most importantly, effective.

This book is a must-read for anyone looking to excel in the real estate industry, whether you're just starting out or have been in the business for years. The book is written in a way that makes something as nerdy as financials and taxes, well, fun, making it easy to follow and implement the strategies outlined. What sets this book apart is its focus on financial success - it's not just about selling properties, but also about building a profitable business.

The authors provide valuable insights and downloads on how to manage your finances and save on taxes, including a list of 100 deductions, and ultimately focus on increasing your bottom line. I wish I had access to this book at the beginning of my career - it would have saved me countless heartaches, headaches, and thousands of dollars. The first year that I hired NW Premier, the team we assembled was able to save me over forty-three thousand dollars in taxes and they were able to stop the IRS from sending me the nasty letters that I was beginning to receive.

I highly recommend 'The Financial Blueprint for Real Estate Agents' to anyone looking to take their real estate career to the next level, and highly recommend taking this subject seriously as it means everything in business and in life. Financial security is not something to take lightly.

Thank you, Nathan and Mike for making your life passion available to everyone.

Aaron Heard-
MAPS Coach
Top Producing Real Estate Agent

Table of Contents

Foreword

I took a personality profile test 15 or so years ago when I first started at Keller Williams Realty, and the person who gave me the test said, "When you see a spreadsheet do your eyes glaze over?" My response was, "Yes!"

I think most realtors feel this way - we are sales people! We love people and design, and typically don›t love numbers, or even understand them a lot of the time. I know there are exceptions to every rule, but I am no exception. After getting hit with a six figure tax bill two years ago, I implemented a few of Mike and Nathan's strategies to make sure it didn't happen again, and periodically check in to evaluate expenses and adjust. After doing just one of the strategies recommended, I got a $180K tax credit over five years. Mind blown.

A little more financial history - back in 2007 and 2008, I made every possible financial mistake: I spent it as fast as I made it, I didn't save money for taxes, and ultimately when the market changed, I owed back taxes and was in a financial mess. I took Dave Ramsey's Financial Peace Class and really changed the way I did things. That helped, but it was very basic. I paid my taxes, saved a lot, bought investments, etc. I definitely rebuilt my financial portfolio as well as my real estate team. But there was no strategy involved.

After the record year I got hit with a huge tax bill and talked to Nathan about my options for never having that happen again, I added in several options and feel much more comfortable with my finances knowing I have NW Premier in my corner. We always hear about the uber-rich hardly paying anything in taxes, and I know they are using some of the strategies in the book.

So, as a twenty-year real estate veteran who has made many of the mistakes outlined in this book, and also been the recipient of amazing financial advice from Nathan and Mike, I am telling all real estate brokers out there that you can't afford NOT to read this book. It's like someone offering you money and not taking it. You will increase your wealth if you implement even some of these things.

I am so grateful not only for this book but the service and advice I have received over the last few years. I wish I had learned these things earlier in my business and love passing along what I have learned to my team and other brokers.

Nathan does a great job breaking things down to make them understandable, and has a fun writing style that makes this book an enjoyable read. I highly recommend this book to not only new realtors but long-timers as well!

Amy Asivido
Principal Broker in
Oregon and Washington

Introduction

We are so glad you are here! Really. The fact that you are opening this book means you have taken the life-changing and adrenaline-packed jump into the world of business ownership, and we couldn't be more excited for you. If you are anything like we were, you are experiencing a wild cocktail of emotions. The excitement of supreme optimism is often followed by an intrinsic gnawing that you're not enough. This can be an intense up-and-down ride. It's the ultimate game of chicken and the commission is the bait.

While you embark on your new journey, it is important to recognize the reality of your situation. Approximately 87% of real estate agents fail within the first five years of being in business. In our experience, one of the main reasons agents fail is due to poor understanding of running a business and keeping business finances. Without accurate numbers, agents are unable to plan appropriately and unknowingly make destructive decisions. Oftentimes the business plan is simply not significant enough to provide the life someone envisioned. If agents do not know their numbers like conversion ratios and profit margins, the cost of running the business can be significantly more than expected and lifestyle can take a massive hit. What is equally as shocking is the reality that gross commissions **DO NOT** equal personal income.

Understanding and mastering the difference between gross commission income and personal income can be the catalyst for unimaginable success.

Gross commission income (total commissions earned) - Business Expenses (*all* the expenses required to make your business run) = Personal Income.

EXAMPLE

GCI	$257,000
Business Expenses	-$142,500
Personal Income	$114,500

All of this actually makes sense. Most agents don't get into the business because they love numbers, profit margins, taxes, and financial statements. Nope. Instead, most agents love the work, the people, the schedule, and the income. Real estate agents engage in a business that provides a lifestyle in which they can spend their time doing what they love with a tremendous amount of flexibility in the calendar. What few will tell you is that while your calendar is within your complete control, this business will put a demand on your attention no matter where you are or what you're doing. It is an all-consuming thought to start, grow, and execute a thriving real estate business.

There are tremendous amounts of resources vying for your attention that boast all sorts of miraculous results. So, we decided that instead of blowing piles of smoke to distract you from the mediocrity of the actual results, in this book we will simply tell you how to get shit done. No secrets, no gimmicks, and no gatekeeping knowledge. Our primary objective is to ensure you have the knowledge needed to run a financially successful business, keeping as much of your hard-earned money as possible. Do you want to know unique tax planning tips so you can pay the least amount of taxes possible? Done. Do you want to know how to increase your income?

Done. Do you want to know the mistakes we see the majority of real estate agents make with financial reporting? Done. Do you want to know how hundreds of agents are keeping more of their hard-earned money so you can too? Yes? Then this book is for you.

We are here to help you as you embark on this journey of business ownership. We've done it, and we've done it successfully. It started when I (Nathan) decided to do something different and asked my coworker, Mike, to join me. We left our familiar jobs in financial services and founded NW Premier in 2019. We had a simple goal: help real estate agents keep more money in their pockets. Agents are sold so much shit that it can be hard to make sense of all the options and make a good decision. Our primary objective was and is to be a profit center for agents and give back to agents who are working diligently and creating so many wonderful things for themselves and their communities. That is what fuels our mission. Our mission is to be the go-to, trusted financial advocates for real estate agents, independent contractors, and small business owners.

And to be completely transparent, we are damn good at what we do. We save people thousands of dollars; dollars for them to spend on increasing their quality of life. That is what inspired us to write this book. We want to get this knowledge and these strategies into the hands of the public - because if you (yes, I mean YOU) succeed, our world succeeds. We want you to be able to live the quality of life you desire. We want you to be able to go to work, love your job, and know that you are helping people when you use your skill sets to help them buy or sell a home. That is what it comes down to for us, and that is why this book is in your hands now.

Many real estate agents enter the industry to enjoy the autonomy of setting their schedules and earning unlimited commission-based income. And those things are wonderful and valuable. However, running a successful real estate business requires a transition from being a trusted salesperson to a world-class business owner. This transition often requires the development of new skills.

When agents become business owners by default rather than by design, they are propelled into business ownership, typically unprepared, and ultimately face many decisions and difficulties.

For example, when dealing with tax complexities you begin asking questions like:

What taxes do I pay and when?
What is a CPA?
Why do I need bookkeeping?
What's the difference between a CPA and a bookkeeper?

You are now navigating legal structures. You'll have to address things like:

What's an LLC?
Why would someone be taxed as an S-Corp?
How do I even set one up correctly?
What does "personal liability" mean?

The operations of the business are now under your full control. Have you thought about:

How do I hire and pay employees?
What insurance do I need?
What does my state require of me?

Questions like these are perfectly normal for new business owners and many agents enter real estate without ever hearing these questions or obtaining this knowledge. Even brokerages often fail to provide operational guidance. It's not exactly their job. Most agencies focus on maximizing gross commission income (I wonder how **they** get paid...) and very few adequately teach how to maximize personal income. (I wonder how **you** get paid...) That's where we come in. They help you make it; we help you keep it.

This book aims to give you the confidence to make informed decisions that benefit your business. By the end, you'll understand:

- How to structure your business entity correctly
- Which taxes do you owe and how to pay them on time
- Essential accounting and bookkeeping practices
- Steps to avoid common mistakes that can cost you dearly

With this knowledge, you can run your real estate business with focus and peace of mind. You'll know exactly what systems and procedures you have in place and why - all aligned with your goals for the future.

Real estate offers independence, flexibility, and unlimited income potential. But without the right foundation, even top producers can struggle financially. This book provides a financial and operational blueprint to help you achieve long-term success in your real estate business.

We couldn't be more excited to share this with you. If you'd like to learn more about our company and the services we offer, please scan the QR code on the following page. We look forward to serving you.

Nathan Ganz
Mike Ross

SCAN THIS QR CODE TO SIGN UP FOR EXCLUSIVE RESOURCES THROUGHOUT THIS BOOK.

Chapter 1

Welcome to Business Ownership

"The way to get started is to quit talking and begin doing."

Walt Disney

1.1 Time to come out of your cocoon. The Journey from Real Estate Agent to Business Owner

Hey! Welcome to the Financial Blueprint for Real Estate agents. Would you ever guess that you'd be here? You know, reading a book about how to set up and run a profitable business as a real estate agent? I'm guessing some of you are still in shock that your friend convinced you to get licensed while others of you have been doing this for 20 years and want to learn all you can to advance your business and profitability. Either way, you have opened this book and we couldn't be more proud of you! You've taken a risk into a way of life that very few will ever experience. You are one of those rare people who are living life by design on your own terms. Well done!

The fact is real estate agents are business owners. No matter why you got into business ownership, whether it is something you've always wanted to do or is the natural biproduct of your new career, here you are. To be fair, most real estate agents do think of themselves as business owners but have no actual context for what that means. Being a business owner means that the buck stops with you. End of story. You are the driving force of your income, responsible for legal and professional compliance while keeping excellent financial records. Your ability to learn and adapt standard business practices like goal setting, creating and executing business plans, and building a network of professional help will often determine how successful you are financially.

It is not always easy to know if you truly think of yourself as a business owner. In fact, it can be quite tricky to quantify. So let us clarify this for you. After working with hundreds and training thousands of real estate agents we have learned that the most obvious sign an agent has successfully transitioned their brain to "business owner" is that they make a clear distinction between gross commissions and personal income.

Gross commission will *never* equal personal income. There are necessary expenses incurred in the creation and continuation of your business that come out of your gross commissions before it gets realized as income. The first expense is usually just getting licensed. The cost of your books, classes, materials, and tests are all valid business expenses. These expenses are used to lower your taxable income and ultimately give you clarity and insight into the revenue required to run a successful business that can pay you what you're worth. As your business grows, there are different options and strategies to maximize these deductions to best benefit your specific situation. We will discuss tax deductions at length later.

In addition to being the driving force of your company, being a business owner means taking on a variety of responsibilities that go beyond selling homes. You are now responsible for managing your finances, marketing your services, and maintaining relationships with clients and other industry professionals. Excited yet?!

If you're more overwhelmed than excited, you're in good company. We have worked with hundreds of agents and every single one of them needed help. Even the wealthiest have had areas of waste and confusion. It's our passion to remove both of those hurdles and see agents thrive on their way to financial success.

It's interesting to note that the more financially successful an agent gets, the more likely they are to hire a coach. A growing agent could sidestep unnecessary pain by strategizing how to get a coach as soon as possible and just freaking listen to them. Wouldn't that make a lot of sense? It's our experience that successful business owners love sharing their wealth of knowledge when they feel someone values their impartation. So be humble and receptive and see what might happen.

Agents who develop a sustainable and profitable business do so with a clear vision of where they are going, strong communication skills, a positive attitude, and a willingness to go above and beyond for their clients. Within this book you will learn to develop a network of help by displaying expertise, building trust and rapport, and maintaining those relationships over time. A network of help should include, but not be limited to a title rep, mortgage advisor, financial advisor, CPA, and NW Premier.

At NW Premier we have created a large network of help by consistently engaging with other professionals, finding those who share our values and align with our mission. It has taken countless hours meeting with and interviewing CPAs to find a couple of firms who are unified in mission and committed to partnering for our client's best interest. It is insane to us how much of that industry is based on compliance and not actual tax planning or help. That said, it is never a waste of time to build your network. You can monetize your network by offering value above and beyond the average agent. Besides, average won't cut it in the days to come. Average will not give you the life your future self is enjoying. Excellence is mission critical and developing a world-class network of help will initiate the space for prosperity at the highest level.

If you are lacking a world-class network of help, prioritize taking time to get introduced to your mentor's resources, or start by asking for recommendations on Facebook or LinkedIn. You can absolutely do this. Once you do, you will find yourself being valuable in a way that few ever experience, and prospects and clients will value your efforts tremendously. And who knows, maybe that connection you've nurtured will turn into a new income stream for you as well. You'll never know unless you ask.

1.2 Responsible Business Ownership (and other oxymorons)

Successful business owners will parrot the same thing over and over again. And what do they say? "Know your numbers!" If you don't understand the basic financial principles that guide each and every decision you make, then each financial decision has a reduced likelihood of being optimal. Successful business owners know their numbers so they can consistently make optimal financial decisions. It's not good enough to just know what the numbers are, it is critical that you have a working understanding of what they mean.

In our business, Nathan is far more the numbers guy and Mike—well, Mike's a sales guy. He's not even interested in the numbers, really. He just doesn't care what we paid in processing fees or utilities. And yet, Mike can recite the financial fundamentals of the business masterfully even though he doesn't care to dig into the accounting or bookkeeping. You need to be able to do something similar. In order to make optimal financial decisions you must have a working understanding of your business' financial fundamentals.

And yet, numbers aren't everything. Beyond the numbers exist motivations, missions, goals, strategies, passions, and a world of creative marketing opportunities so you can have the life you deserve.

Wouldn't it be great to know if your marketing strategy is even working, though? And if that would be helpful information, how would you get the answer? How would you know? How do you pivot? How are new market conditions affecting your profitability? How much should you even spend on marketing? Every agent will have a world of advice for you but how do you know what is right for YOU? If you don't understand your numbers, you'll likely never know.

Let's look at what an efficient marketing spending plan looks like. From our experience, the most skilled agents use less than 10% of their gross commission income for marketing. That means that every $1 spent on marketing produces at least $10 of revenue. If an agent does not track their expenses in contrast to their income, they have no clue if their efforts are producing the best results possible. I (Nathan) have spoken to so many agents who have no idea where their money goes or how effective their spending is. Instead, they just tell me "I have money in my bank account, so I feel like I'm good." That attitude is a slippery slope to financial ruin. If just one thing doesn't go as planned, these owners are at risk of financial failure. That is completely avoidable for an attentive owner. You'll often find experienced agents who signed up for marketing services and have never tracked the results years deep in an auto-pay situation that is producing the equivalent of a dissipating mist on a hot day. It's basically worthless.

Here is how you determine what percentage of your income is being spent in a certain category. Let's use marketing as our example. Take the total amount of money spent in marketing and divide that by your total gross commission income. The result will be the percentage of your revenue spent on marketing. See the two different examples below:

Marketing	$9,300
Gross Commission Income (GCI)	/$105,000

Percentage of GCI = 8.8%
(Within appropriate range.
Consider spending more to make more.)

Marketing	$14,400
GCI	/$105,000

Percentage of GCI = 13.7%
(Outside appropriate range. Consider making changes.)

1.3 The Importance of Financial Management for Real Estate Agents: Live. Laugh. Love. All the way to the bank

We will make this as clear as possible: if you don't manage your finances, you won't have finances to manage. That's the simple truth. Every bit of planning starts with tracking. Tracking calls, closing ratios, referral trees, and finances are all necessary components of a successful business. Long-term sustainability in business always comes back to tracking and understanding your finances. Money is the fuel that runs the mothership, and without proper cash flow, businesses crash. Therefore, financial management becomes the foundation on which all profitability is built.

Financial management is the ability to accurately track your finances, look at future wants and desires and create a plan to achieve them all while remaining profitable in the here and now.

Understanding this fundamental financial principle is so helpful for making optimal financial decisions. The information provided by effective financial tracking allows agents to make informed decisions about their business. The numbers provide visibility and clarity to what is working and what can be improved.

There is and always will be the sales aspect of your job. That will never go away. It's often all the other things that impede progress. In order to avoid delays, we recommend that each agent has a working knowledge of every aspect of their business. Agents need to know enough information to make educated decisions and should not overanalyze an aspect of the business they can outsource.

For example, you probably don't need to know every in and out of QuickBooks to make savvy financial decisions; however, agents would benefit greatly from hiring an exceptional bookkeeper like those at NW Premier and learn how to read their financial reports. That way, the clarity provided by tracking isn't useless. Instead, the clarity provided elicits a positive impact on decision-making.

1.4 Setting the Stage for Financial Success: Curtains Up

I've never met a real estate agent who has said, "I'm content with not meeting my financial goals." But, if that's you, you might as well throw in the towel now and go home. Because financial success is not built on settling, it's not built on average, and it certainly isn't built on being just "okay" at your job. To set your life up for financial success, you must gladly take the responsibility of being in the driver's seat of the car, navigating road hazards, and preparing for detours. So, lock in your destination, blast that road trip playlist and lets fucking go.

You know how you hear all these amazing stories of successful agents and wonder to yourself, *"How can I do that? Why is my business not reaching that level of financial success?"* THIS IS A GREAT QUESTION! And the truth is that you CAN do it, and following the steps in this book will assist you in ensuring financial results. No agent needs to fail – especially you. It's all a choice in how you approach your role as a business owner.

Key Questions

1. Am I fully dedicated to being a successful real estate agent and business owner?
2. How can I determine my level of commitment?
3. How can I adopt a business owner mindset and apply it to my real estate business?
4. What specific actions can I take to think more like a business owner?
5. Which aspects of business ownership will be the most difficult for me to handle as a real estate agent?

Action Items

1. Evaluate your level of commitment to being a successful real estate agent and business owner. Identify any areas where you may need to increase your dedication and develop a plan to do so.
2. Research and implement specific actions to adopt a business owner mindset, such as setting clear goals, developing a business plan, and tracking financials.
3. Identify the aspects of business ownership that will be most challenging for you and create a strategy to address them. This may involve learning new skills, outsourcing tasks, or seeking help from a mentor or coach.

4. Find someone to hold you accountable for your strategies and check in with them regularly to ensure you are staying on track toward achieving your goals.

Chapter 2

Entity Shopping: Finding that perfect fit

> "Truly successful decision-making relies on a balance between deliberate and instinctive thinking."
>
> *Malcolm Gladwell*

Now that you own a business, you get the wonderful privilege of figuring out how you want to file your business with your Secretary of State and the IRS. Of course, the IRS cannot advise you even though they know exactly what would be best for you. Thanks, Internal Revenue Service! What a pleasure it is to do business with you!

An entity is nothing more than how the government views your business. With each entity type, there are advantages and disadvantages for agents. Each entity provides unique protections, has different tax forms, and makes sense depending on the nature of your business. There are several types of entities. In this section, we will only go over the most common types of entities for agents.

Sole proprietorship - a business owned and run by one person, with no legal separation between the owner and the business.

This is the default entity type for every person who earns a 1099 income.

Partnership - a business owned and run by two or more individuals, with profits and liabilities shared among partners.

Limited Liability Company (LLC) - a hybrid business structure that combines the benefits of a partnership and a corporation, with owners having limited personal liability for the company's debts and obligations depending on state regulations.

S Corporation - a type of corporation that provides the limited liability benefits of a traditional corporation and can limit self-employment tax.

Corporation - a separate legal entity from its owners, owned by shareholders who elect a board of directors to manage the company.

Because there are several advantages and disadvantages for each entity type, we have identified four areas to consider when making an entity decision:

1. Taxes: Consider the tax implications of each business entity, including the tax rate, deductible expenses, amongst other factors. For example, an S-Corporation might be more effective at lowering self-employment taxes than a sole proprietor.

2. Operational Costs: Consider the costs associated with setting up and operating each business entity, including legal fees, accounting fees, registration fees, and other fees.

3. Management Structure: Consider the management structure of each business entity, including the level of control and involvement you want in the business, and whether you'd like to work alone or have a partner.

4. Business Growth: Consider your future plans for business growth and expansion, as some business entities may be better suited for this purpose.

To make sure you have the best chances, have a consultation with someone who knows these entity types like the back of their hand. The proper advisor can help you determine which business entity is right for your specific needs and circumstances by helping you weigh the pros and cons of each option so you can make an informed decision.

Below is a high-level view of each of these entities so you can begin the process of determining which type is best for you.

2.1 Sole Proprietorship: Simplicity and Personal Liability

Sole Proprietorship (also called sole prop, independent contractor, or 1099 income earner) is the most common and the "default" entity type for businesses. It is the simplest of all the entity types because you already are one. When I was a kid, I would mow lawns and get paid for it. Simply because I worked and received income turned me into a sole proprietor. If an agent gets licensed, they are already a sole proprietor without any additional effort. You do nothing. You do not typically have to file anything with your state (besides your Real Estate License), and you can track your expenses in whichever way seems best to you. Taxes are filed under your social security number, and business income and expenses are documented on a fancy form called a Schedule C. That's where you tell the IRS which deductions you are claiming.

Because of the sole prop entity structure, kids like me who mow lawns can now deduct the gas they use, the mower they purchased, and the traveling expenses required to perform the job, to name a few. They can do all these things without any additional complications. The same rules apply with a sole prop in real estate. All business expenses are valid and deducted from your taxable income without much effort.

You can view a sample schedule C here:

Sole proprietors have unlimited personal liability. They are responsible for all the debts and expenses of a business, and personal funds are typically available in a lawsuit. To paint a picture, let's say you are showing a ton of houses in one day. The middle of the day comes around and you all stop to get your favorite Mexican food, and, since you're no stick in the mud, you all decide to get margaritas as well. Your lunch goes exceptionally well, and you are all ready for the afternoon agenda. On your way to the next showing, you encounter a major problem. You just got in a car crash and it is your fault. So now you have a client in the car, you have alcohol in your system and the wreck was your fault. Can you imagine how that would feel? Oh man, it would be awful. But the pain doesn't stop right there. What does the victim of the accident do in this case? They bring a lawsuit and pursue financial restitution.

In this scenario, what finances are available in a lawsuit?

Well, as a sole proprietor, all your bank accounts, including joint accounts, are fair game. Your real estate, if owned personally, is subject to creditors. Investment accounts and personal property are available as well. In some states they graciously limit how much can be taken out of bank accounts but what's left often still leaves a person completely devastated. For example: Iowa will allow a creditor to take all a person's money except $100. What the fuck is $100 in the light of a financial disaster? Other accounts like retirement accounts and life insurance cash value have unique levels of creditor protection depending on the state. Some states protect these accounts from creditors at 100%. These are great features that can protect a sole proprietor facing a financial loss.

Because sole proprietors have unlimited personal liability, we recommend purchasing an umbrella policy from your property and casualty agent; AKA: the person who insures your home and auto. These policies are inexpensive and very effective. They come in increments of $1,000,000 and usually cost around $15-$25 per month per million. We strongly recommend purchasing a million dollars above your net worth. If your net worth is $2,356,000, the proper policy should be at least $3M.

So, take a moment right now to consider the level of personal liability you are comfortable with. Does your desired personal liability protection line up with the protection options afforded as a sole proprietor?

2.2. Partnerships: Shared Responsibilities and Risks

While sole proprietorships are the simplest business entities to set up and manage, they offer no personal liability protection. To mitigate risk and share responsibilities, some real estate professionals opt for partnerships. This is basically a marriage contract, so listen up.

Partnerships are businesses owned and run by two or more individuals, with profits and liabilities shared among partners. This structure not only allows for shared responsibility but also shared risk. Each partner brings their unique skills and expertise to the table, which can contribute to the success of the business. The negative is that you must be in business with someone else. It takes an exceptional level of communication and commitment to create a prosperous partnership.

Therefore, it is essential to choose the right partner and establish clear expectations, standards, and responsibilities. This includes deciding how profits and losses will be divided, how decisions will be made, and how conflicts will be resolved.

Partnerships can be wildly effective in the right situation. One of our top producing clients has a partnership and they enjoy the ability to discriminate profit sharing and reduce personal liability. Partnerships provide all the same tax deductions as sole proprietors while having decreased personal liability.

2.3. Limited Liability Company (LLC): Flexibility and Protection

You're probably well aware of the importance of protecting your personal assets from any potential liability. I mean, who buys a house and doesn't buy insurance on that home? While sole proprietorships are the easiest business entity to set up, they offer no personal liability protection. Instead, additional insurance is required to protect against personal liability. For those who want limited liability protection supported by the local and federal government, that's where LLCs come in.

LLC stands for Limited Liability Company, and it's a popular choice among real estate agents due to its flexibility and protection. As the name suggests, an LLC offers limited liability protection, which means that your personal assets are separate from your business assets. This can be extremely beneficial if your business were to be sued or face any legal issues. Remember the car wreck scenario? Let's see how that would go as an LLC instead of a Sole Proprietor. Instead of all the bank accounts, houses and investments being available, only the assets of the business are available. That is a huge difference!

The benefits of an LLC don't stop there. LLCs also offer flexibility in terms of management and taxation. Unlike other types of entities, LLCs can be managed by the owners themselves, or by a designated manager. Additionally, LLCs have the option to be taxed as other entity types, such as an S-Corp. S-Corps are designed so that the owner can get paid as an employee and an employer, often lowering self-employment tax. Profits or losses are passed through to the owners and reported on their personal tax returns. That's why an LLC is considered a "pass through entity". On December 31 of each year at 11:59pm whichever profit or loss is in the company passes through to the owners' personal tax return.

Each state treats entities for agents differently. For example, in Oregon, the LLC provides almost no legal protection for agents, whereas just a few miles south in California, the Department of Real Estate does not recognize an LLC as a legal entity for agents. Instead, CA agents can file as a C-Corp structure and elect to be taxed as an S-Corp to avoid double taxation. Topping off the west coast, Washington state allows agents to file as an LLC without any issues. Since details shift from state to state, be sure to verify with your state regulations before determining the best option for you.

Of course, with any business entity, there are some drawbacks to consider. For example, forming an LLC can be more complex and expensive than forming a sole proprietorship. Additionally, there may be ongoing fees and requirements to maintain the LLC status. Keep in mind, these are all tax-deductible expenses to your business. Whatever it is, go in with eyes wide open.

In our experience, when an LLC is accepted by the state, that is our preferred entity type every time. They are egregiously simple to create and provide such excellent legal protection and flexibility that it just works time and time again.

Keep in mind that an LLC in and of itself provides no tax benefits at all. This is a huge misunderstanding in the real estate community. We often hear agents say, "I know! I need to get an LLC because I pay too much in taxes." And this just simply isn't true. By default, every LLC is taxed as a sole proprietorship. As your business grows your LLC can elect to be taxed as a different entity type. However, the initial purpose is protection, not tax efficiency. So, since there is no tax benefit but there is a massive liability benefit, when should an agent get an LLC? As soon as they get their license! Non-negotiable. If you need an action item from this book, go get yourself the legal protection that is in alignment with your personal liability preference.

2.4 S-Corp election: Reducing Self-Employment Taxes

Have you ever met an agent who is an S-Corp? Have you ever wondered why they chose an S-Corp over other options? Ever wondered when is the right time to switch to an S-Corp? Well, then this chapter is for you.

When we meet agents who are using an S-Corp election we often say "That's great! What led you to do that?"

I'd say 9/10 agents respond with "My CPA told me to do it."

Ok Got it. "And how does it help you?"

They tend to smirk and say, "I have no idea." We laugh about it and then I ask, "Well, would you like to know how it helps you?" and they always say yes.

An S-Corp is a tax election, not the entity itself. This is an important distinction. Someone can have an LLC or a C-Corp and elect them to be taxed as an S-Corp. So, the first step to using this option is to have an entity that allows for its election.

The main value to using an S-Corp over an LLC taxed as a sole proprietorship is a reduction in self-employment tax. Self-Employment tax is currently 15.3% above your income taxes. This is a significant tax that many 1099 earners don't know they even pay. This tax pays for things like social security and Medicare.

As a sole proprietor, you're responsible for paying self-employment tax up to a predetermined taxable income limit. This limit changes every year. In 2023, the limit was $160,200, and in 2022 it was $147,000. This self-employment tax is a massive drain on your wealth building so we have major vested interest to reduce it and its impact. On $160,200 of taxable income, there is $24,510.60 of Self Employment Tax. Uh... no thank you.

Self Employed Agent:

GCI - $250,000
Expenses - $100,000
Taxable Income = $150,000
Current Self Employment Tax = $22,950

After hitting that magical $160,200 (2023 law) of taxable income, guess what happens? Are you ready for this? You're going to love it. You still have to pay 2.9% in self-employment taxes forever, on every earned dollar above that limit. Good times, right!?

But there is good news: by electing to become an S-Corporation, you can likely reduce those pesky self-employment taxes and keep more of your hard-earned money. Here's how it works:

instead of getting paid one way (1099), you'll now be able to get paid in two different ways. The first component to your income is called a "salary."

The salary is the amount you'd pay someone on a W2 to do your job. And that can be really tricky.

I mean, let's be honest, real estate agents do several jobs all at once. You're a master negotiator, counselor, administrator, social media expert, marketer, salesperson, and the taxi all in one! The IRS is helpless in determining how much an S-Corp member's salary should be. The only direction they give us is that the salary portion of your income must be "reasonable compensation." What the fuck does that even mean? There are several schools of thought, but a specific answer for your situation should be well thought out and strategically aligned to your tax and wealth-building needs.

One idea is to go to salary.com, search your city and job title to find the median income. As of the date of this book, salary.com says that a real estate agent in Kansas City, MO has a median income of $44,450. Whereas in New York, NY, the median income is $53,256. This could be a good launching point to help determine your salary. We still recommend working with a tax professional to make your best decision. Just a thought.

Now remember, you want to do all you can to keep a salary justifiably low because a salary in an S-Corp still has that nasty 15.3% tax on it. Except this time, they have changed what it is called. In a sole proprietor, the 15.3% is called "Self-Employment Tax." However, in an S-Corp, that 15.3% tax is called "Payroll Taxes." They are the same taxes paid to the same places for the same amounts at the same time but now that you're an S-Corp the names of the taxes change too. You know, just to confuse you. Why would the IRS want to make it easy?

Because you must be paid "reasonable compensation," you can't just pay yourself peanuts to dodge taxes. One of the reasons you must earn a reasonable compensation is because the other way you get paid is more tax efficient. After your company has revenue and pays expenses including your salary, whatever is left is called "profit." Profit is awesome! Every financially successful company has a profit. It's a good sign you are producing excellent revenue and keeping expenses in check.

One of the great benefits to profit is that there are no payroll taxes! That's a 15.3% savings on every dollar that ends up in profit instead of salary up to the annual limit. After that the benefits aren't as noticeable, but they certainly matter. A 2.9% reduction in taxes above the annual limit is still helpful.

Let's look at our agent again, this time as an S-Corp.

S-Corp Agent

GCI - $250,000
Expenses - $100,000
Salary - $50,000
Profit/Distribution - $100,000
Current Payroll Taxes: $7,650

Sole Proprietor	S-Corp Agent	Difference
S.E. Tax - $22,950	Payroll Taxes: $7,650	$15,300 Savings

This is just one component of how a top-producing agent can keep more of their hard-earned money. I hate hearing people say, "I don't want to make more money because I'll pay more in taxes." This is completely untrue.

First of all, each dollar is only taxed at the rate of the income pertaining to that particular tax band.

2023 Federal Tax Brackets			
Tax Bracket/Rate	Single	Married Filing Jointly	Head of Household
10%	$0 - $11,000	$0 - $22,000	$0 - $15,700
12%	$11,000 - $44,725	$22,001 - $89,450	$15,701 - $59,850
22%	$44,726 - $95,375	$89,451 - $190,750	$59,851 - $95,350
24%	$95,376 - $182,100	$190,751 - $364,200	$95,351 - $182,100
32%	$182,101 - $232,250	$364,201 - $462,500	$182,101 - $231,250
35%	$231,251 - $578,125	$462,501 - $693,750	$231,251 - $578,100
37%	$578,126+	$693,751+	$578,101+

So in this example let's take a single filer. Only the money between $0 and $11,000 gets taxes at 10%. No matter how much they make. One person could make $20,000 and another person could make $2,000,000. Regardless, the first $11,000 for both of them will be taxed at 10%.

For those who continue to make more money, only the money from $11,001 up to $44,725 gets taxed at 12%. And so on and so forth. The higher bracket has absolutely zero effect on the income in previous brackets. By averaging out all the brackets, you get what's called your net effective tax rate. So if someone earns enough money to be in a higher tax bracket, not all of their money gets taxed at the new rate. Only the money in that participating bracket gets taxed at that percentage.

All you have to do is take your total tax liability and divide it by your taxable income and you can get your net effective tax rate or, simply put, the average tax on every dollar you earn.

For example, if I have $25,000 of taxable income, here's how it would play out:

10% tax band - $0-$11,000 = $1,100 of income tax
12% tax band - $11,001 - $25,000 = $1,800 of income tax

Total income tax ($2,900) / Total taxable income ($25,000) = 11.6% net effective tax rate.

This means that every dollar earned in this scenario has 11.6% of income tax associated with it. The more money this person makes, the higher the net effective tax rate. At least, that is the common knowledge surrounding tax bands.

That said, when someone makes more money, it's like giving a carpenter more than just a hammer. They have options. They can be more creative. They have the tools to create whatever they can imagine. For us, when we have clients who need every dollar to survive, it's like taking tools away and it greatly limits our ability to be creative and find tax-efficient solutions. However, once someone starts making more money, more and more opportunities to reduce taxes begin to be in play.

We currently recommend using the S-Corp election when your taxable income is around $60K-$70K. There are a few reasons for this. Filing as an S-Corp is usually more expensive as it requires an additional tax return (1120s), payroll, and most CPAs recommend a specialized bookkeeper. Please verify with your tax professional. If you're looking for a way to reduce your tax burden and keep more of your hard-earned money, it's definitely worth considering and talking about.

So, the next time tax season rolls around, don't let self-employment taxes weigh you down. Electing an S-Corp status may just be the strategy you need to get them off your back for good.

2.5 Corporations: A whole different level

If you're looking for a business entity that offers even more structure and protection, a corporation may be the way to go. A corporation is a separate legal entity from its owners, meaning that it can enter contracts, own assets, and incur liabilities on its behalf. This structure provides even greater personal liability protection than an LLC.

But, as with any business entity, there are trade-offs to consider. One of the biggest drawbacks of a corporation is the complexity of its structure and management. Corporations are required to have a board of directors, officers, and shareholders, as well as adhere to strict rules and regulations. This can make corporations more expensive and time-consuming to set up and manage than other types of entities. And let's face it, for most of us the more complexity we encounter, the less we execute. It's paralysis by analysis.

Another important consideration when forming a corporation is the tax implications. Corporations are taxed as separate entities, which means that they file their tax returns and pay taxes on their profits. This can lead to what's known as "double taxation," where profits are taxed at both the corporate level and the individual level when they are distributed as dividends to shareholders.

However, corporations also have some unique tax advantages. For example, they may be able to deduct certain expenses and may have lower tax rates on their profits than individuals. Additionally, corporations can offer different types of stocks, which can be beneficial for raising capital and attracting investors. Most agents will never need a business this complex. And yet it is still beneficial to understand them. The more you know about business, the more informed and accurate your decisions will be.

Overall, forming a corporation can be a smart choice for real estate professionals who are looking for a highly structured and protected business entity. Especially if your business is going to be raising lots of money from several investors.

2.6 Choosing the Right Entity Type for Your Situation

Picking the right entity can be like picking a life partner so take your time and understand your commitments. It is clearly important to understand each option and see if it's compatible with your business and future objectives. This means keeping in mind these important factors and what they mean in the context of the entity you choose.

Here are some business terms that you'll want to understand so you can make an informed decision.

Revenue - the total income generated by a business.
Expense - the cost incurred in running a business.
Profit - the excess of revenue after expenses.
Asset - anything of value owned by a business.
Liability - a financial obligation owed by a business.
Cash flow - the movement of cash into and out of a business

Balance sheet - a financial statement showing a business's assets, liabilities, and equity, a snapshot of every financial decision the business has ever made.
Gross profit - total revenue minus the cost of goods sold.
Net profit - total revenue minus all expenses. Also known as your net income.
Return on investment (ROI) - the amount of return on an investment, expressed as a percentage of the investment's cost.

Be sure to review all your options and weigh the pros and cons. It is a big decision, and you may want to consult with tax or business consultants (that's literally what we're here for). Choose wisely, my friends!

Key Questions

1. How does picking an entity type impact your business?
2. Which entity factor (i.e. protection, tax planning, simplicity) matters the most to you?
3. What is the impact if you change nothing?

Action Items

1. Research the tax implications of each business entity, including the tax rate, deductible expenses, and other considerations that may impact your financial situation.
2. Consider the costs associated with setting up and operating each business entity, including legal fees, accounting fees, registration fees, and other operational costs.

3. Evaluate the management structure of each business entity, including the level of control and involvement you want in the business, and whether you'd like to work alone or with a partner.

4. Plan for your business growth and expansion and consider which business entities may be better suited for this purpose.

Chapter 3

Cash is Trash, Cash Flow Is King

"Making more money will not solve your problems if cash flow management is your problem."

Robert Kiyosaki

Most agents are understandably focused on generating income and building their business. And they should! There's nothing wrong with that. It's just that sustaining a great business takes more than charisma and rugged good looks. Cash flow and asset building are not just some shiny objects of conversation, they are both crucial to short and long-term success. In this chapter, we'll explore the power of cash flow and asset building, and how they can help you achieve financial security and long-term prosperity.

3.1. Cash flow inspection report, understanding the foundation of your business.

At its most basic level, cash flow is the movement of money in and out of your business. You can determine cash flow trends by tracking the money you are generating and the money you're spending. That said, cash flow is about more than just balancing your books each month. The act of balancing the books or tracking your finances isn't the magical part; you must also use the data to make optimal financial decisions time and time again. The value here is building a sustainable business that generates consistent income and profit over time, not just big commissions and flashy Instagram posts. That shit gets old really quickly.

There are several ways to generate cash flow. First and foremost, consistently having real estate transactions solves many problems. Lumpy, large commissions make month-to-month budgeting and forecasting difficult. The consistency of your work matters greatly. It's one thing to get four sales in a month and wait three more months for another banger, and another thing to get a sale once a month and radically improve your cash flow. Having consistent cash flow promotes lower stress and the pursuit of better financial habits. So that said, what would it take for you to get 1 sale per month? How about two? What can you do to consistently create revenue? Whatever you do, consistency in marketing, networking, advertising, and closing will solve the vast majority of issues created by stagnant cash flow. Getting money into your business brings life. And living things grow.

There are other ways to create cash flow besides buying and selling real estate. For example, you might also focus on building a portfolio of rental properties or investing in businesses that generate steady income. There's no formula here. The idea of diversification is somewhat misleading. The wealthiest people I know spend most of their time on one thing or one industry. Their efforts are not minimal or divided. Instead, they almost hyper focus on building the business into a real asset. I like the way Robert Kiyasaki defined an asset: "Assets put money in your pocket, whether you work or not..." Essentially, an asset is something that pays you. Whatever your strategy, the key is to focus on building assets that generate cash flow over and over again.

Again, an asset is something that pays you. A liability is something you pay. There may be seasons where an asset feels like a liability until it starts paying you. Your real estate career might be a part of that. When you started, it was all you could do just to get a sale and pay some bills let alone travel the world. But over time, your business with all your branding and marketing, truly becomes an asset full of positive cash flow.

3.2 Proactive Cash Flow Planning - You're playing chess not checkers.

Starting a career in real estate is an investment that requires upfront costs. You'll likely want to purchase marketing materials, build a website, and more. Not only that, but there's also a good chance that three-six months will pass before receiving your first commission check. As a result, financial metrics should be discussed before you even begin. Have you counted the cost of starting? Have you included excess savings for unexpected expenses and opportunities?

Until an agent is established, we always recommend having six months of income set aside. A lot of places will say "expenses" should be set aside, but we all know those are unpredictable. So, six months of income is the safer bet.

When it comes to excellent cash flow it is always good to ensure expenses stay below your income. It might sound exceptionally basic, but it needs to be said. It clearly needs to be said because we are a society riddled with debt and real estate agents are no exception. The allure and pressure that comes with your career choice is a real force. It will require focus and determination to avoid the pitfalls of unproductive debt.

The fastest way to get ahead financially is to increase your income without increasing your lifestyle. And one of the biggest mistakes we see is when agents earn a large commission check and leverage it to buy a payment. We all know that one agent who can't keep cash in their pocket and spends it all on their latest toy. This is a recipe for disaster. Instead, get used to having that money in the bank. Think twice before buying something. Calculate the difference between a need and a want. You can do it.

As we've discussed, cash flow is the key to any business, including real estate. You should have profit regularly. Everything stagnant is dying. Finances are no different; if you don't earn money, you can't spend money, and you won't make more money.

Stagnant cash is becoming less valuable every day. Money needs to move to grow. Creating regular sales and excellent cash flow ensure that your business stays healthy and profitable in the long run.

3.3 Roller Coaster Income with no brakes.

Inadequate cash reserves, unexpected expenses and inconsistent income are common cash flow challenges facing real estate agents. Let's face it, this career is notorious for having unpredictable income. It's wise to have adequate cash reserves or other cash-flowing assets to weather any downturns in the market or unexpected expenses.

One of the tried and tested ways to address this challenge is to simply create a spending plan and stick to it. Understanding your income and expenses helps you identify areas where you can cut costs and create a strategy for building your cash reserves over time. A spending plan gives you complete control over every dollar that floods into your business. The old term was "budget." But we hate that saying for entrepreneurs. It feels so restrictive. Can't you just hear that crotchety old employee mindset creeping in saying, "We can't buy that. We must stick to the budget"? GROSS. Instead, give yourself control over your money by creating a plan on how you'd like to spend it and what it will do for you. If your priority is to create cash reserves, *you* have the power to make those decisions. Don't let anyone convince you otherwise.

In fairness, not all decisions directly result in saving more money. A spending plan might recommend $1,000 for marketing this month. However, a situation has presented itself and you see an unparalleled opportunity to spend money in a way that could be very advantageous to your business and create more income. In a budget-style system, you just don't spend the extra money because the budget is like a financial god, and you do not go against it. With a spending plan system, your options live and breathe, giving you the authority and autonomy to make real-time decisions regardless of preconceived restrictions. If you're going to move to a more flexible spending plan, just make sure you're being honest with yourself. Will it really make you money to buy a prospect's $500 dinner? What is the opportunity cost of that dinner? What did you give up that you could have done with that money if you hadn't spent it on that dinner? These are the decisions we all face regularly if we are to keep a spending plan that produces excellent results.

Therefore, it's not about restricting the spending of money to a magical number or percentage. No. Creating a spending plan allows you to live and breathe with the ebb and flow of your market. Again, check-in and make sure you're being honest with yourself. It can be a tricky game of wants vs. needs.

We mentioned earlier that another strategy is to focus on building assets that generate consistent cash flow to supplement your amazing career. By investing in rental properties, for example, you can generate steady income even during times when your real estate business is slow. Similarly, investing in dividend-paying stocks or businesses that generate consistent income can help you build a reliable stream of cash flow over time. These assets can often be the difference between having a long-term career in real estate or having to give up your dream to pay bills. Smart entrepreneurs see the potential ways a business can fail and spend ample time addressing and eliminating as many risks as possible in order to avoid financial failure.

Having no cash flow is a major problem when growing a business. So, if you're not creating cash flow by buying and selling, it may make sense to create another income stream. Many books boast that everyone needs seven or more income streams. We are not a proponent of a particular number. Like we said, some of the wealthiest people we know got there because they had tunnel vision on their mission, and they had a singular focus. We are simply saying that you can be successful in this career through many paths and one of them might include insulating your income in downtimes by creating other assets that create consistent cash flow.

3.4 Poor Expense Management and Tracking - Don't worry! If you make enough money all your problems will go away, right?

Cash flow flourishes when we pay attention to it. Effectively tracking and managing expenses eliminates costly mistakes and provides insight to the financial health of your business. Without a clear understanding of your expenses, it can be difficult to make informed decisions about your business and make the most of your income.

To address this challenge, simply use a system for tracking your expenses. This might include using accounting software to categorize your expenses and generate reports, or simply keeping a spreadsheet of your expenses and income. At NW Premier we require all our clients to have QuickBooks online and use dedicated business bank accounts and or credit cards. QuickBooks online will connect to your already existing bank accounts and update every 24 hours. If an agent uses dedicated business accounts, it makes tracking so much simpler and more accurate, and thus the reports are actually useful.

Once you have a system in place for tracking your expenses, the next step is to manage them effectively. This means identifying areas where you can use your money more efficiently without sacrificing the quality of your work. For example, you might look for ways to reduce your marketing expenses or streamline your administrative tasks to free up more time for revenue-generating activities. We know several real estate agents who have started to use virtual assistants or a company like ours to ensure they are getting the best help for the best price. This also frees up their time to create more money and that's always good.

When an agent does their bookkeeping, that activity does not directly produce revenue. They will hopefully use that information to make decisions, increase revenue, and create profitability, but the act itself of categorizing expenses and tying out loans produces absolutely zero results. There comes a point very quickly in which leveraging other professionals and freeing up your time for actual income-producing activities is mission-critical. If it takes you five hours a month to do your bookkeeping, could you make more income with an extra 60 hours a year than it costs you to have a bookkeeper do it for you? If so, hire them (us).

It is also important to stay on top of your expenses and regularly review your spending plan to ensure that you're on track. This might mean setting aside time each week or month to review your expenses and income or working with a financial advisor to develop a more comprehensive financial plan. If your bookkeeper gives you monthly financial statements and you are not reviewing those documents, what good are they?

By managing your expenses effectively and tracking them closely, you can gain a clearer understanding of your cash flow and make more informed decisions about your business. This can help you achieve greater financial stability and build a sustainable real estate business over the long term.

Key Questions:

1. What is cash flow, and why is it crucial to your long-term success?

2. What are three things you can do to address your specific cash flow challenges?

3. What system will you use or create to accurately track your finances?

Action Items

1. Develop a strategy for generating consistent cash flow, such as selling properties more consistently, building a portfolio of rental properties or investing in businesses that generate steady income.

2. Create a spending plan and stick to it to ensure you have adequate cash reserves to weather any downturns in the market or unexpected expenses.

3. Implement an effective cash flow management strategy to ensure you're making decisions with the most accurate data.

Chapter 4

Dollars and Non - Cents: Common Financial Tracking Mistakes

"We are all born ignorant, but one must work hard to remain stupid."

Unknown

I think we all agree that financial literacy in our country is low. In our experience, the real estate industry is not better, and may be even worse. Just think about it. You take a bunch of passionate salespeople and thrust them into business ownership without any financial criteria or curriculum. The odds of a real estate agent having a world-class understanding of their finances is rare. We are going to show you how to change that.

To make wise financial choices, you need accurate data and a meaningful understanding of what that data represents - areas many agents struggle with. Mistakes in this area can cause serious problems, increased taxation, or business failure. What good is it to put all this effort into building a booming business if you are not capitalizing on the financial reward? It's like we say around NW Premier all the time: we don't mind spending money, but we absolutely hate wasting it.

4.1 Incomplete or Disorganized Record Keeping - It's time to take the clothes off "that chair".

Incomplete or disorganized record keeping can be a significant challenge for real estate agents looking to build healthy cash flow and financial stability. Without accurate and organized records, it is nearly impossible to understand your income and expenses, track your progress toward your financial goals, and make informed decisions about your business.

To address this challenge, successful agents develop a system for record-keeping that works for them. This might include using accounting software like QuickBooks, keeping a detailed spreadsheet of your transactions, or working with a bookkeeper or accountant to manage your financial records.

Whatever system you choose, the key is to be consistent and diligent in your record-keeping. This means you must record all your income and expenses promptly and accurately and keep your records up to date regularly. A good sign you may need to leverage a professional is if you get behind and cannot use your record keeping as a key part in decision making. It comes down to the best use of your time. And as often happens, the best use of time is not in detailed financial tracking. Go figure.

In addition to developing a system for record-keeping, it's also valuable to stay organized. This might mean keeping physical or digital copies of your receipts and invoices or using a filing system to keep track of important financial documents. We highly recommend keeping a digital copy of your receipts. There are several apps that you can use to take pictures of your receipts so they stay clean and organized. And, as a massive bonus, you don't have to keep a box of papers in your closet. Win-win.

The reason you need to keep receipts is not for the deduction itself. Receipts are there to validate the legitimacy of a business expense in an audit and verify the accuracy of accounting.

Business owners typically don't get in trouble over the validity of the expense, rather they usually get in trouble over having no supporting documentation for the expense. The IRS wants to know several things to validate an expense.

Imagine you're taking a prospect or client out to lunch to discuss business. You'll need to capture the itemized receipt itself that shows the name of the restaurant, the date of the meal, and the amount of the meal. You'll also want to write on the top of the receipt notating who you were with and what you discussed. It could be as simple as writing: "Mike Ross: bookkeeping." This will help validate the expense to the IRS and keep your record keeping clean.

4.2 Like The Offspring says, "You Gotta Keep 'em Separated"

One of the most important pieces of advice for any business owner is to keep personal and business finances separate. When personal and business income and expenses come out of the same account, this is called "commingling funds." Commingling funds is a recipe for financial disaster. Here are the top reasons you should avoid commingling:

- It makes accurate record-keeping and accounting nearly impossible. Unraveling personal and business expenses can be like trying to organize sand. You're just never going to get it right.

- You lose visibility into the financial health of your business. You cannot measure key metrics or identify problem areas.

- It makes complying with tax rules incredibly challenging. The IRS expects businesses to have separate books and accounts.

- It increases the risk of personal liability. If your business runs into debt issues, creditors may be able to pierce the corporate veil and come after your personal assets.

- It makes planning and decision-making difficult. You cannot assess your business's cash flow or implement sound financial strategies.

Proper financial separation is a key step to running a successful business. You should open separate bank accounts for your business, get a separate credit card, and use accounting software to track finances separately.

This section aims to drive home the importance of avoiding commingled funds at all costs. In the subsequent chapters, we will provide strategies to help you properly separate your personal and business finances in practice.

Establishing a strong financial foundation now will pay dividends for your real estate business in the long run. Proper separation of funds will make your bookkeeping, tax filings, and financial planning exponentially easier - and potentially save you from serious financial trouble down the road. This is a standard business practice and a non-negotiable for our clientele.

4.3 You're not an Ostrich, Don't put your head in the sand.

Keeping track of your financial metrics and performance indicators will have a humongous impact on your success. While numbers can be daunting, understanding what they mean and how they can help you make informed business decisions is worth all the trouble. That said, creating a system to track your financial metrics is only useful if you actually use that information to make good financial choices. If you're not stress-testing your business plan and adapting it based on your goals and performance, you're missing out on valuable insights. One of the costliest mistakes we see regularly is when clients think, "Oh, I'm so glad they ran these numbers for me, that was nice," instead of actually using the numbers to adjust their business practices. When you're dating someone, you tend to look for red flags. We look for those in businesses too, and if you are not consulting the numbers for your business, that is a HUGE red flag.

To keep your business in balance and avoid unnecessary debt, visit your metrics regularly and adjust your business accordingly. For those who are just beginning, reviewing every quarter makes more sense as there is typically not enough data, and transactions are lumpy. For more consistent and seasoned agents, a thorough monthly review is recommended. How great would it be to take one day a month to go over your current results against your business plan to ensure you're doing all you can to succeed? Take the time to review, strategize, and prioritize your finances and business plan in the next month. So many agents work **in** their business, and they fail to work **on** their business. Think of financial metrics as guardrails that keep you on track and help you hit your goals. If you are bowling with the guardrails up, you may not hit a strike, but you will sure as hell hit at least one pin.

One extremely helpful tip is to review your profit and loss report as a percentage of income instead of just dollar amounts. When businesses have lumpy income saving a particular dollar amount may or may not be enough. Let's say I want to save $2,000/mo. I want to save $2,000/mo because that would reflect 10% of my annual income going towards savings. And, on average, that would be accurate. But let's say I go out and close a massive deal and I earn $45,000 that month. Is saving $2,000 still enough? Absolutely not! So instead of using a static number, save a percentage. That way, regardless of how lumpy your income is, you always save the right amount.

Establishing and tracking key performance indicators (KPIs), such as closing ratios and profit margins will give you a direct insight into the direction and success of your business. By understanding what drives your business forward, you can set income goals and sales targets that are achievable. For example, if you want to make $100k in personal income and your profit margin is 40%, you'll need to make $250k in commissions. Most agent's business plan to the wrong number under the false assumption that commissions = personal income, but it does not. By reviewing your performance indicators regularly, you can determine how many listing appointments you need to set each week to reach your income goal. Don't be afraid to chat with someone more successful to help you revise your metrics and stay on top of the game. Remember, financial metrics are living and breathing documents and should be adapted regularly, at least yearly.

4.4 Financial Projections - X marks the spot. Hidden treasure awaits.

Think of financial projections as living and breathing documents. These documents also adapt to your ever-changing environment. If your projections are inaccurate, you're essentially aiming at the wrong target. That's like playing pin the tail on the donkey, blindfolded, and spinning around three times after taking a shot of tequila as a friend points you in the wrong direction. Good luck! It doesn't make sense, and it's not going to get you anywhere meaningful.

Accuracy is key when it comes to financial projections, and there's no shame in seeking help from a professional. They can help ensure that your projections are on point, so you can make informed decisions that will move your business forward.

On the other hand, outdated financial projections were once right, but now they're about as useful as a cassette tape in a world of streaming music. It's time to re-engage and update them to reflect your current situation. Remember, you don't want to work solely in your business, but also on your business. That's how you'll know if you're on track with your goals.

Take the time to write a business plan and get that shit done! If you feel like you've lost your way, take a week off, hire a professional, spend a day with a coach, go see a speaker, or do whatever it takes to get back on track. Accurate and up-to-date financial projections are the compass of your business, so make sure they're solid. Stay disciplined, get motivated and find that treasure.

4.5 Skydiving without a parachute may feel fun until you hit the ground

Okay, let's face it - managing finances isn't the most exciting part of being a real estate agent. But it's a crucial part of running a successful business. When it comes to managing your finances, hiring a professional accountant is key. But not all accountants are created equal, so let's break it down into two groups.

First, there are filers. They're the "meh" option. They're less expensive, usually reactive, and not proactive. You meet them once a year, you give them your documents, they type everything into their computer, and they're done. No questions asked, no opportunity to save you money, no vision casting, no long-term tax planning. Just a short-sighted filing to lower your income from last year's BS. Boring.

Then, there are strategic planners. They're like the cool kids at the CPA dance. They're proactive, they ask questions, and they're always looking for opportunities to save you money. They're typically more expensive but are worth it. Trust us.

Here's the thing: when you hire an accountant, you don't just paying for their services, you also pay for what you could miss out on if you don't have a strategic planner on your team. And the cost of missed opportunities is usually far more than their fee.

Story time. We had a potential client walk into our financial firm years ago who bragged about their super cheap CPA who happened to be their college roommate. This agent had done extremely well, with gross commissions between 200K and 400K annually. Well, this self-proclaimed cheap CPA was certainly a filer. We didn't address the CPA in the first meeting even though we took note of it. However, at our second meeting, I politely pointed out that because their cheap CPA did absolutely no tax planning, this particular prospect had overpaid nearly a million dollars in taxes over the last 20 years. Yeah. A million fucking dollars. Good thing you had that cheap CPA! Well done. All it would have taken was a 20-minute conversation and the slightest bit of strategy to eliminate almost a million dollars of waste.

As you continue to develop your business, be honest with yourself about outgrowing your CPA. Not every CPA is right for every agent in all seasons of their business. Shop around. Find someone you really like and connect with and believe will put the effort into seeing your tax efficiency skyrocket. They should be asking you several questions about your business and what you'd like to see happen this year and the years to come. Good CPAs dig in and want to know your thoughts and feelings as well as the details of your situation. If they don't even ask for your previous years' returns, I'd run away.

Here are some good questions to ask when interviewing CPAs:

- How long have you been practicing and with what clients/industries?

- How do you help clients develop tax planning strategies to legally reduce liability?
- How do you stay up to date on tax laws in my specific industry?
- Besides filing, what additional services do you provide?
- Are you an expert in my industry?

All that said, don't overlook the importance of a professional accountant for your real estate business. A strategic planner can help you make sure your finances are in good hands and that you're taking full advantage of all the opportunities available to you. Plus, they're way cooler than those boring ass filers.

4.6 Profit/Loss Statements - Because Hope Isn't a financial plan.

As your real estate business grows, understanding your profit/loss statement becomes even more crucial. It's a financial report that shows how much money your business has earned and spent over a certain period. By running comparisons year over year, you can see what's working and what's not. You'll see trends and be able to predict the ebbs and flows of business.

To start, look at the top line - your revenue. This represents the money your business has earned over the period covered by the statement. Next, look at your expenses. These are the costs associated with running your business, such as office rent, marketing expenses, and salaries. These expenses should be in categories that reflect the purpose of the expense. Each category has a specific purpose and should be in alignment with sound business practices.

By subtracting your expenses from your revenue, you'll get your net income. If your revenue is higher than your expenses, you've made a profit! But if your expenses are higher than your revenue, that's a loss.

You might also come across some key terms on your profit/loss statement, like gross profit, operating income, and net income.

Gross profit is your revenue minus the cost of goods sold.

Operating income is your gross profit minus operating expenses.

And **net income** is your operating income plus any other income minus any other expenses.

It might seem overwhelming at first, but once you get the hang of reading your profit/loss statement, it becomes easier to understand. And the insights you gain from it will help you make informed decisions about the future of your business.

4.7 Bad ass bookkeepers

Let's imagine you just crushed another year of real estate. You separated your personal and business finances; you have your LLC and life is good. You are busy focusing on selling real estate and doing things you love. Let's be honest, going home and categorizing your expenses isn't exactly the highlight of your day, nor should it be.

I'm sure you got into the real estate business for many reasons, but being a bookkeeper sure wasn't one of them. What exactly does a bookkeeper do anyways? Why would you want to hire one? They're just number crunchers, right?

Unfortunately, that's what a lot of people think. However, that couldn't be further from the truth. It's more than data entry and number crunching. Bookkeepers are the people responsible for providing clarity and transparency into the life of your business. Their work is the foundation for every financial decision you make. The accuracy of their accounting could be the difference in thousands of dollars of taxes. They are like a financial MRI machine. Like we said above, the numbers and data have to actually mean something to you. How are you supposed to grow your business each year if you don't know what it costs to do so? And how can you solve a problem you cannot see?

Let's say you just crushed your best year ever and earned $500,000. You got a taste of the hard work paying off and now you want more. How will you do the same production again if you don't know how you got there in the first place? How much money did you spend on marketing? Taking clients out to lunch? On sponsorships? If you do not know how you got to the best year ever, how are you supposed to repeat it or beat it?

A bad ass bookkeeper is a gamechanger for your business. They take a tremendous amount of pressure off of owners and give them the resources necessary to make exceptional decisions.

4.8 Implementing Best Practices for Financial Tracking "There Are No Shortcuts to Success, Do it right the first time"

Implementing best practices for financial tracking will save you money and grow your business.

We will say this over and over and over and over again: if you have yet to do so, your major priority after finishing this chapter is to separate your personal and business bank accounts. No commingling allowed! If the IRS sees that, it can be cause for further investigation, piercing the corporate veil and becoming a real problem. And let's face it, nobody wants the IRS snooping around your stuff. And besides, you're a business, not a person. So, do yourself a favor and get a separate account for your business. Some credit unions are more favorable for businesses, but if you want simplicity, you can opt to go with a big bank or an online banking system.

We want to encourage you again, please do not wait until the end of the year to visit your finances. That's like waiting until the last minute to study for a test or do your Christmas shopping - not a great idea. Instead, check in monthly. Make sure you're on track to meet your financial goals and adjust your strategy as needed.

Itemized receipts are your friend. Keep 'em, love 'em, cherish 'em. And if you're like us and hate keeping physical copies, try using apps like Cam Scanner or the QuickBooks App to snap a picture of your receipts and keep them organized. Having accurate documentation to support your transactions will solve the vast majority of problems.

Key Questions:

1. What is one area you know you are avoiding in regard to your finances?

2. What steps do you need to take to properly separate your personal and business finances?

3. What key financial metric matters the most to you and how can you best track it?

Action Steps:

1. Open separate business bank accounts and credit cards. Use accounting software to keep business and

personal finances separate. This will make tracking and compliance much easier.

2. Identify key financial metrics to track like profit margins, closing ratios, expenses as a percentage of income, etc. Review these metrics regularly and use them to make business decisions. For example, you may need to adjust your marketing spending plan or set new income targets.

3. Update your financial projections and business plan regularly based on your metrics and performance. Outdated plans and projections will lead you off track. Meet with a coach or accountant if needed to revise them.

Chapter 5

Missed Tax Opportunities - Don't you just love overpaying the IRS?

"Nothing is more expensive than a missed opportunity"

H Jackson Brown, Jr.

Have you ever heard the phrase, "You don't know what you don't know?" It implies a simple truth, which is that none of us know everything, and we must come together collectively if we are to comprehensively understand a matter. Adding to that idea, we need humility to ask for help when we feel that we do not have an excellent grasp of a subject. Well, how true is that regarding the IRS tax code?

The tax code is an ever-evolving document that I imagine very few, if any, have ever read word-for-word. Let's assume for a moment that someone took the time to read every word. What are the odds that the person insane enough to read the entire tax code also possesses the capacity to perfectly apply it to every situation? I'd say slim to none. Wouldn't you? The reality is that tax professionals are all doing the best they can with the information they can obtain and apply.

Instead of trying to learn every nitty-gritty detail of the code, specialists spend their time studying the code that directly correlates to their specialty. Go figure. Using a specialist will increase your knowledge and likely provide you with a more efficient and complete experience. Based on our experience with hundreds of real estate agents, here are a few commonly missed opportunities we think you'll find beneficial. Keep in mind that all of these ideas require confirmation in your specific situation. Please reach out to us at NW Premier or your professional to ensure you are in compliance and maximizing your tax efficiency.

5.1 The Augusta Rule: In honor of those pajama pant zoom meetings

Every agent we have ever met works from home. Most of them take a home office deduction and don't know that there could be another way. In fact, we find that simply formalizing what an agent is already doing can be a great way to increase efficiency. The way we do that is by appropriately using the Augusta Rule. The Augusta Rule is a little-known tax deduction tool that allows any homeowner to rent out their primary residence for 14 days or less in a calendar year without paying taxes on the income earned from the rental. That means you can earn extra income from renting out your home for a short period without having to worry about paying taxes on that income. It's a win-win situation!

For example, let's say you own a home in a popular vacation spot, and you decide to rent it out for two weeks during peak season (while you are sipping pina coladas on a beach, of course). If you rented it for 14 days or less and filed the income correctly, you will not be required to pay any income tax on the money you receive. Your vacation just paid for itself!

For agents using an S-Corp: if you have an office outside of your home (*COUGH* where you hang your license

COUGH), you can use the Augusta rule to your advantage. The Augusta rule will replace your home office deduction which, let's be honest, doesn't usually provide significant tax relief. The home office deduction allows you to take the business use % of your home and apply that to your business in the form of deductions. For example, if your home is 2,000 sq ft and you use 200 sq ft for your home office, you will be able to deduct 10% of several home-based bills. In this scenario, if you had a $300 gas bill last month, $30 of that would be deductible. You multiply the deduction by your net effective tax rate (the average of all your income taxes) and that is your tax savings.

Gas bill - $300

$300 x 10% business use = $30 deduction

$30 x 26.5% (net effective tax rate) = $7.95 income tax savings

As you can see, that is a lot of work for a very small reduction in your taxes. In contrast, let's see how the Augusta Rule works for real estate agents and why it might be a better fit for you. Keep in mind, this is not designed to be an exhaustive list of all the ins and outs of the IRS code. This is to get you interested in an idea that might really help you. We always recommend working with a professional familiar with this strategy to execute it flawlessly.

A couple of things that make the Augusta Rule very attractive is that if you stay within the guidelines of the law, there is no cap on the amount of money you can receive and there is no tax on the money you receive. That's a massive deal! The Augusta Rule only applies to homeowners who rent their primary residence for 14 days or less. If you rent your home for longer than that, you'll need to pay taxes on the income you receive, and the strategy becomes powerless.

There are a few stipulations to this tax deduction. Check to see if this applies to you.

- ☐ You must own your primary residence, and you cannot be renting
- ☐ Your business needs to be an S-Corp and have an EIN
- ☐ You must have an office outside of the home (the brokerage where you hang your license qualifies)
- ☐ You must rent your primary residence for 14 days or less in a calendar year
- ☐ If using the home for a shareholder meeting (recommended) you must keep meeting minutes (see QR code for example)

- ☐ Money must be transferred (cannot just account for it)
- ☐ Must issue a 1099 at the end of the year
- ☐ Recommended having a written rental agreement allowing your S-Corp to rent your home to validate the transaction

So, let's get into how this helps YOU. As an S-Corp you are allowed to rent a space for a monthly shareholder meeting. Who exactly are the shareholders in a single member S-Corp? All of your personalities. Congratulations! They're finally coming in handy. Because this is a shareholder meeting, you'll need to keep monthly meeting minutes and issue a 1099 form for renting your home.

The rent money gets paid from your business to your personal bank account and is categorized as rent which is 100% deductible. The income gets filed as non-taxable rental income on your personal tax returns. I want to be abundantly clear that this is not just some accounting strategy. You actually have to have the meeting. You cannot just say you did. That's not how this works. Please, whatever you do, don't lie to the IRS. It's just not worth it. We can be creative all while staying within the plain black and white of the tax code.

Think about this, how impactful would it be to take one day a month to work ON your business instead of just IN your business? Imagine taking one day a month to go over your finances and your business plan, meet with your mentor or coach, strategize for the coming months, delegate responsibilities, and actually run your business. For real, what would the impact be? Think about it. Right now. At this moment. Take inventory and visualize what your business could look like if you took one full day a month to increase yourself and your business. How much better could you perform if you took the time to know your business on a world-class level?

Most agents work from home already. This strategy simply formalizes what you are already doing at home and provides better tax efficiency for it. The way to get started is simple; schedule one meeting per month on your calendar. Keep the meeting. Fill out your meeting minutes and start getting paid.

Now that you've scheduled your meetings, we need to figure out how much you can get paid. It can be challenging to figure out how much to pay yourself because there are no official guidelines. There are a few ideas about how to determine the amount you should pay yourself. Here are three options we see often in the marketplace:

1. Comps: You can call comparable spaces in your area and get rental prices. From recent court rulings, this seems to be the most justifiable option.

2. A generally accepted rule is to take three zeros off the value of your home. For example, if your house is worth $750,000 you can rent your home for $750/day.

3. Whatever you think is "reasonable." Because there are no clear guidelines, you can do whatever you like. That said, we highly recommend keeping within a genuinely reasonable framework. Let's be honest, you know what's reasonable and what's not. If you think you're being too aggressive or conservative, you're probably right.

If you rent your house for one day per month, that equals 12 days for the year. That schedule means you still have two more days to stay under the 14-day annual limit. For those other two days, you can use your home to host a party, event, or other business-related function, and "rent" the home as an event space for your business. Once the event becomes a formal business expense, you'll be able to write off several costs associated with the event like food, drinks, plates, clean-up, and more.

Take this real-life example: we have a client who hosts a wildly fun and well-attended Friendsgiving party each year. Since several clients and prospects attend their Friendsgiving, they decided to formally turn it into a business event and use one of their two remaining Augusta rule days. In order to get some ideas on rent costs, we called several restaurants and caterers to determine how much it would cost our client to rent a comparable space and provide similar food items. We took the average of all the comps and were able to justifiably apply a $3,500 rental check for the event. That's $3,500 out of their business tax-free while doing what they've always done but now they're getting the tax credit for it. Not only that, but they were also able to deduct the food costs as well. How amazing is that!?

These ideas aren't just some gray-area mythical concoction. No, these are creative strategies hidden in plain sight within the black and white of the tax code. You can absolutely save money on your taxes and keep more of your hard-earned money. It takes a small adjustment in your strategy and thinking for your financial life can get radically better in a hurry. The important thing for you to remember is that this strategy, in particular, must be done ethically and in good faith. DO NOT LIE. Document everything religiously and make sure you have valid reasoning behind everything you do. If you think you're being shady, you're being shady.

5.2 Hiring your Minor Children: what are child labor laws, anyway?

Some strategies just have a financial impact. This one feels like there is so much more to it. We have clients who want to hire their kids as an income-shifting strategy only and forget about one of the most important factors, you get to work with your kids! What an opportunity! They get to see you running your business and you have the chance to inspire them to think differently and, most likely, have a much better financial start than you did. The impact of hiring your kids can go far beyond tax savings, it can be the catalyst for generational wealth.

The basic idea is to transition income from a high-taxed individual to a low-taxed individual all while maintaining some control over the money. If you can accomplish that, you have successfully made more money and are taxed less. Have we piqued your interest yet?

If you have a healthy income, pay too much in taxes, and have kids under the age of 18 who are not on your business's payroll, that needs to change now. Go to the bank and open a bank account for each of your children. Since they are minors, who else has to be on the account? That's right. YOU! Every time you pay your children for legitimate work they do for your business, that income goes right to their bank accounts and is a valid tax deduction for your business. By putting your children on the payroll, you lower your personal income and reduce your personal income tax. Instead, that income is credited to your child, and they pay the income taxes. This is where the savings come into play.

Currently, income tax is not taken on the first $13,850 that any individual earns in a calendar year. That amount is called a "Standard Deduction" and it is adjusted every year. Nobody, whether they make $100,000 or $1,000,000, pays income tax on income below the standard deduction. So, if you put your children on the payroll for $13,850 in 2023, you are not only getting an excellent deduction, but you are also shifting income from your high tax bracket to a lower bracket, ideally a 0%, income tax bracket.

The major downside to hiring your kids in an S-Corp is that the income is still subject to payroll taxes. Do you remember how much that is? That's right, 15.3%. In this scenario, you, as the employer, pay 7.65% and your child, as the employee, pays the other 7.65%. If you've ever had a W2 paystub before, you'll see the separation of you and your employer's payroll tax contributions.

EXAMPLE: Paying minor children in an S-Corp

Child Payroll: $13,850
Payroll Taxes: $2,119
Income Taxes: $0

If you want to take the tax benefits of hiring your kids to the next level, you could even consider starting a family LLC that is taxed as a sole proprietor. By doing this, you can hire your children within the family LLC and even eliminate the payroll taxes, which means that there will be no payroll tax or income taxes paid by your kids as long as the income stays under the standard deduction. In this scenario, the family LLC will invoice your real estate company for whichever services are rendered. The invoice is 100% deductible to your business. The family LLC receives the income and distributes it to the employees (your kids). This one extra step will even get rid of the 15.3% payroll taxes. When done correctly, this can truly be tax-free money.

EXAMPLE: Paying minor children in a Sole Proprietorship

Child Payroll: $13,850
Payroll Taxes: $0
Income Taxes: $0

Sometimes it takes the smallest number of changes to make a big impact. By adding one extra step, this hypothetical family reduced their tax liability by an additional $2,119/child/year for sending an invoice once a month. Do you see how having all the tools makes a big difference? You can, in fact, make more money and pay less in taxes.

In real life, we have a client with three minor children who all work in the business but never got paid before meeting with us. When we recommended formalizing their efforts, our clients were shocked at the results.

All three kids legitimately work in the family business. The family LLC invoices their real estate S-Corp for $3,000/mo for services rendered. The family LLC deposits the money and pays each kid a $1,000/mo salary. That adds up to $36,000 for the year! That's $36,000 of MISSED DEDUCTIONS. We simply formalized what they were already doing.

This client has a high net effective tax rate and, by executing this strategy, saved themselves over $12,000 in personal income taxes and another $5,508 in payroll taxes by hiring their kids through their family LLC taxed as a sole proprietor. When it was all said and done, they were able to radically reduce their tax liability and keep control of over $17,500 of their hard-earned money. That money would have gone directly to the IRS but now it is staying within their family. We absolutely love that! This is a huge win for this family.

When it comes to hiring your own kids, it's almost like labor laws do not exist. You can hire them to be your assistant, take pictures, be a model, make copies, or, like my 12-year-old did for four and a half hours a few days ago, put things through the shredder. It does not matter what you hire them for, it only matters that you hire them, and they actually do the work. Again, we are completely against lying to accomplish some mystical accounting objective. Make them do the work. Overpay them if you want. Give them a signing bonus to incentivize them to work hard. Whatever it takes, get the kids involved. Remember that this isn't just a tax strategy, it's a valuable lesson that can pay massive dividends for the rest of their life.

Our assumption is that you spend money on your kids. Big shocker. There's always something to spend money on, whether it be school clothes, summer camps, sports programs, art supplies, video games, and that trip to leave them at Grandma and Grandpa's for a week this summer. Thank God for the occasional break, right? Whatever it is, wouldn't it make sense to spend tax-free money on all these things instead of after-tax dollars? Since you pay your kid and you still maintain some control over the bank account, you can help your kid spend their money appropriately. You're still their parent. You still have your name on the account and your input matters.

As amazing as this idea is, it can be somewhat restrictive. Unfortunately, this only applies to immediate family. Grandparents, aunts, and cousins cannot hire your kids and receive the same tax benefits. It has to be your minor children to apply.

5.3 Cost Segregation Studies: What's wrong with 30-year-old carpet?

One of the incredible benefits of real estate investing is that you can depreciate an appreciating asset. This is unique because every other financial item I can think of is depreciated when it loses value. However, for real estate, you can depreciate the asset (except the land, you can never depreciate the land) while it's appreciating in value.

A cost segregation study is a great way to accelerate depreciation on a property. It involves breaking up the house into smaller sections and giving each section its own depreciation schedule. For example, carpet depreciates on a certain schedule, while paint, roof, HVAC, and electrical all depreciate at a different schedule. The traditional way to depreciate a real estate investment is collectively over a specific period, usually 27.5 years. With that said, who wants to lay down on some cozy, dust-infested 27.5-year-old carpet? That's a big NOPE for me. It is not hard to realize that carpet naturally depreciates more quickly than the structure (unless the carpet is glued down. Then, for tax purposes, it magically becomes part of the structure.) and you should get credit for that.

Depreciation allows you to take that reduction of value against your income on your taxes. You're allowed to make the property less valuable on paper because the items used to build it become less valuable over time. This wondrous accounting principle begins to take your taxes behind the woodshed all while your home likely increases in value in the real world. This creates a tax utopia. The result is significantly more tax-efficient income and profit. In some cases, it can eliminate the taxes completely. We get excited about that shit around here!

We have a client who originally reached out because they had a major tax liability and wanted some input. After doing our initial consultation, we learned that this client had a few rental properties. We simply asked if they had already done a cost segregation study and they said they had not. After discussing the strategy with them they decided to move forward, and we introduced them to someone to execute a cost segregation analysis.

Once the cost segregation company did all their work, they were thrilled to tell us they found an additional $185,000 in new deductions by accelerating our client's depreciation. That saved our client almost $70,000 in income taxes that year. If you are a real estate investor we highly recommend looking into this idea. It can be very powerful.

Using depreciation can also be favorable when it comes to borrowing from financial institutions. Most lenders put depreciation back into your income in order to qualify you for lending. They can do this because depreciation has very little, if anything, to do with cash flow. It is an accounting principle. It is not a bill that you pay and therefore does not impact your ability to repay debt. Depreciation can lower your income and income taxes and still not handcuff your borrowing power.

Later on, we will discuss the difference between active and passive income for real estate agents. Once you understand that concept, that seismic lightbulb moment will happen, and you'll want to invest in real estate like never before.

5.4 "Move it or lose it, sister!" - Lloyd Christmas

There are hundreds of potential tax deductions you can claim as a real estate agent. Agents are constantly working, and many everyday items can become deductible. A few common tax deductions that real estate agents miss out on are below. We have also created a tax deduction cheat sheet for you to enjoy! See the QR Code below.

1. Deduct travel by "wrapping": If you are traveling, you can combine business and pleasure, so long as you have an income-generating reason to travel and document the business purpose of the trip. One of the ways this works is when you work on a Friday, enjoy your Saturday and Sunday, and then work again on Monday before heading home. Imagine you travel to Hawaii to meet with a brokerage or client. You can wrap the weekend in meetings on Friday and Monday and the entire weekend now becomes deductible. Be sure to keep detailed records of your expenses and the business purpose of your trip to support your deduction. Again, no lying. Do what you say you're going to do.

2. Annual S-Corp shareholder meetings: If you operate your real estate business as an S-Corporation, you can have an annual shareholder meeting offsite. By doing

a shareholder meeting, you can deduct the costs of the shareholder meeting as a business expense, including travel and lodging. Just be sure to log everything correctly and keep records of the business purpose of your trip.

3. Streaming services: You can deduct the cost of streaming services like Spotify or Netflix if you use them for continuing education or other business purposes. For example, if you listen to real estate podcasts or webinars on Spotify, you can deduct the cost of your subscription.

4. Cellphone: If you use your cellphone for business purposes (who doesn't), you can deduct the cost of the business use.

5. Vehicles: We get asked often about vehicles and you can absolutely get tax benefits for having a business vehicle. We won't get into all of the details here because they can be nuanced. That said, there are a couple of strange rules you should be aware of.

   First, you can decide to use miles or actual expenses for your vehicle. You cannot do both because the mileage reimbursement has already factored for depreciation. However, you still need to keep track of your miles either way. Tracking miles between personal and business clarifies the business use percentage of all your expenses. In our experience, under the current tax code, using the expense method is more advantageous.

   Another little quirk about vehicles is that you cannot deduct a car payment, but you can deduct a lease payment. If you lease you are simply renting, and leasing is a legitimate business expense, even if it's leasing a car.

> If loan payments were deductible, it would disincentivize people from purchasing cars with cash. However, since cars can be depreciated, those who borrow money and those who pay cash all get the same tax benefits. When leasing a vehicle, you cannot depreciate the vehicle because the owner (bank/dealership) uses that tool on their behalf.

Scan the QR code to see 100 deductions for real estate agents. Use it as a cheat sheet. Anything on this list should be going through your business account and being deducted as a business expense.

5.5 You Wouldn't Hire a Plumber to File Your Taxes Would You?

Let's face it: in the world of taxes, you still don't know what you don't know. And let's be honest, learning the ins and outs of tax law can be a full-time job in itself. As a busy real estate agent, your time is better spent doing what you do best - closing deals and working with clients. That's why the most successful business owners surround themselves with advisors, mentors, and experts who can provide insight into areas where they may not be as strong.

We geek out about finding money for our clients. We hope you're just as inspired to geek out in your own business and become an absolute tax-saving beast. Become your own advocate. You can do it. Now that you've learned so many cool tips, what will you change? How will you take this information and apply it to your specific situation? Again, what will the effects be if you do NOTHING?

Chapter 6

It's Time for Your Annual Check Up - And We're Not Talking About Your Doctor.

"I knew exactly what to do. But in a much more real sense, I had no idea what to do."

Michael Scott

6.1. Like A Ship Without A Rudder

As Zig Ziglar famously said, "If you aim at nothing, you'll hit it every time." And let's face it, hitting nothing is not exactly a recipe for success in any venture, much less as a real estate agent.

Without a plan, you might as well be wandering around in the dark with a blindfold on, hoping to stumble upon success. And while that might work for some, it's not exactly a reliable, repeatable strategy. Instead, a good business plan should be your guiding light, leading you toward your goals and helping you avoid the pitfalls along the way. A good business plan will provide clarity as you face difficult decisions and can often give you the confidence needed to get through challenging seasons. There's just something about knowing where you're going and believing you can actually get there that provides tremendous resolve.

There are several ways of creating a business plan. In fact, you can go online right now and see template after template. But how do you go about creating a good business plan? I mean, how do you even know what a good plan is?

Here are a few good questions to ask yourself about your business plan:

1. Can you envision it?

   If you can see it, you can be it. If what you see excites you, keep moving forward. If a business plan doesn't get you absolutely filled with anticipation and enthusiasm, start over.

2. Is it specific?

   Ambiguity is not your friend. Specific metrics and specific goals are critical to your success.

3. Is it actionable?

   All thinking and no doing produces nothing worthwhile. Good plans provide a clear roadmap to success with actionable steps along the way.

4. Is it objective?

   Business plans are not about how you feel you did. Nope. They are like a plumbline ensuring each goal is subject to accountability. You *want* to be judged by it. Run to that level of accountability, and never run away.

5. Is it challenging?

   A business plan should scare you a bit. If you can accomplish your plan without needing the plan, that's not much of a challenge. Make yourself think beyond what you previously thought was ambitious and push yourself to go to new places.

Everything starts with a clear vision of your future self and what you want to achieve in the coming years. So, take a moment to think about your ideal life. Ponder what your future self is doing that your current self is not. Note the differences. Notice the change in your emotions. Observe who you have become. Growing up, I had a youth pastor who used to always say "You have to be who you're supposed to be so you can do what you're supposed to do." How true is that? Everything starts with being. The doing comes from that place of certainty about yourself. When we focus on doing instead of being, life lacks meaning and is therefore incomplete. Feel who you are to become and use that vision to create a roadmap for your business plan.

Take time right now to start imagining what life will be like for you when you accomplish all you've set out to do. Feel the sense of pride in your soul of a job well done. Feel the certainty you've created in your body and spirit. What is the difference between who you are and who you want to be? What does your future life feel like? Where are you? What are you wearing? Who are your peers? What does your bank account look like? What does it feel like to walk into a room? What is your posture like? How do you breathe? How do you talk? What do you talk about? Who is in your life? Who is NOT in your life? What habits have you adopted? What habits have you left behind? Think. Vision. Feel. Vividly imagine what your life looks like in one year, five years, 10 years. Experience it in your mind before you experience it in life. Go deeper in your thoughts than money and metrics. Feel who you are going to be. Dream. Imagine. Be bold. Be brave. And now rest in that vision of who you truly are.

Now that you have identified who you want to be, you can think about what you're going to do and design a blueprint for success.

6.2. Setting Financial Goals and Objectives for the Year Ahead - Aim for the stars. You might just hit the moon.

With a clear vision in place, you can now set financial goals and objectives for the year ahead. And we're not talking about vague, pie-in-the-sky ideas like "I'm going to sell 100 houses this year," when you sold 20 last year. Instead, objective metrics and accomplishments provide phenomenal feedback to track your progress and ensure that you're actually growing, increasing, and thriving. Sometimes it's easy to be comfortable if there is money in the bank. But is that really "success"?

By using data from previous years, you can set measurable and achievable goals that challenge you but are still attainable. And, while it's important to aim high, you also need to be somewhat realistic. A good business plan should have core objectives, goals, systems, and methodologies to accomplish and execute those goals.

Almost every real estate agency I have been around provides some sort of business planning template or class for their agents. These classes are typically taught by team leads or brokerage managers who have varied levels of expertise in this area. The teaching is inconsistent, sometimes even within the leadership of one brokerage. I've seen some wildly contradictory ideas from high-level leaders. It just goes to show that you can get information from anywhere and figuring out what's real can be challenging.

One of the major errors I see with agencies teaching business planning is that they tend to focus on the wrong number. A significant number of business plans I see in a brokerage focus on GCI (Gross Commission Income) as the key factor. Why is that? Why would a brokerage focus on Gross Commissions? Well, how do most brokerages get paid? On which number? That's right! The gross commissions. So naturally they want that number as high as it can go.

However, which number matters most to the AGENT? Is it the GCI or the personal (NET) income (GCI - EXPENSES = PERSONAL (NET) INCOME)? That's right! Personal income. Agents care about what they get to keep. Agents care about the money they get to use for their family, lifestyle, experiences, and wealth building. That's the number that really matters: the NET INCOME.

For example, if I am a real estate agent and I have a Gross Revenue of $250,000 and I have $150,000 of expenses I am left with $100,000 of personal (NET) income.

AGENT A:

GCI - $250,000
Expenses - $150,000
Personal (NET) Income - $100,000
Profit Margin - 40%

Let's say that I have found a way to increase my profit margin and I can now be AGENT B. In this scenario I have less commission but look what happens:

AGENT B:

GCI - $150,000
Expenses - $50,000
Personal (NET) income - $100,000
Profit Margin - 66%

What are the differences here? The major differences are the GCI and profit margin. Agent A requires $0.60 for every dollar to operate their business. Agent B requires $0.33 for every dollar to operate their business. This is a major distinction. The glaring similarity is that personal income is the same.

So, here's the big question, which option would be better for your family? Income-wise, they're both the same, right? Then which one would the brokerage prefer? AGENT A, of course. The agencies really see no direct benefit from helping you keep more of your money, but they certainly have a vested interest in helping you make as much as possible. And that's not so bad, is it? However, the quality of your life is radically impacted by the amount of personal income you receive, not the amount of revenue your business creates.

I have a friend who was worth millions on paper and had an eight-figure revenue business and they still went bankrupt. Just because a business has strong revenue, does not mean they are making any money. I've seen businesses spend $1.5M to earn $1M. It's a simple math problem with a disastrous ending. Financial illiteracy is a ticking time bomb, and many agents are in a similar spot. They earn big commissions and then buy payments. Then, when the next big commission check gets stalled, they are financially hamstrung because their entire business model was inefficient and healthy personal financial habits were never implemented.

Let's try something different. Let's create a business plan for real estate agents that starts with the amount of personal income an agent wants to make. If agents did this more often, they would realize they typically need to produce more GCI than they thought, and agencies would be happier because the GCI would naturally increase.

When focusing on personal income GCI increases because the amount of personal income needed to live a particular desired lifestyle is always more than someone expects. In America, we are constantly bombarded by world-class marketing. Marketing is nothing more than the art of discontentment. And this discontentment has led us to a place where we have absolutely no context for how much money it takes to support a lifestyle.

When someone tells you they make X amount of dollars you can envision what their life might be like. If I told you about my friend who takes home $500,000 a year, can't you think of what kind of house they might live in? Can you imagine their vacations? Can you imagine what their bank account looks like? Can you imagine their life? Of course you can! Now what if I told you they make $75,000 a year, can you see their life as well? What about $1,000,000 a year? Can you see that too? Yep! We all can. That's how this brilliant marketing machine works.

Think for a moment if your view of that lifestyle is ACTUALLY supported by that income. I suggest that the odds are basically 0%. In fact, the existence of consumer debt validates this idea tremendously. The existence of consumer debt shows me that a person's desired lifestyle is beyond what their income can support.

When we receive an income, we pick a lifestyle we feel is supported by that income. We do this by default. It is almost subconscious. That's one of the reasons it's so hard to get out of the ol' rat race. Just yesterday I saw a commercial about a young woman who got a new job and the first thing the ad recommended her is to buy a brand-new car. Yep, that's an actual commercial! The actress barely gets through telling her mom that she got a new job and she's already leveraging her future income to buy a new car, which she obviously deserved. Yet the reality is that when income proves to be insufficient, we are forced to introduce debt as a way of keeping up with our fabricated idea of reality.

So, instead of focusing on GCI which does not necessarily equate to personal income, focus on personal income and the GCI will skyrocket. It's a win-win.

Let's say, for example, that someone wants to earn a certain amount of personal income. How would they create a business plan with this financial metric in mind?

Here are the key numbers you'll need to know to make this business plan come to life:

Average Commission - Take your previous year's GCI and divide it by the number of transactions in that same year.

______________ /	______________ =	______________
Previous Year GC	Annual Transactions	Average Commission

EXAMPLE: Previous Year GCI $138,000 / 22 Annual Transactions = $6,272.72 average commission

Closing Ratio - How many prospects do you need before you close a sale? How many listing appointments do you need before you get a listing? Keep in mind that this is not just everyone you know, it's representative of the number of actual conversations you have about buying or selling a home with a qualified prospect.

_______________ / _______________ = _______________

Qualified Prospects	Annual Transactions	Closing Ratio %

EXAMPLE: 57 Prospects / 22 transactions = 38.5% closing ratio

Profit Margin - What percentage of your revenue becomes personal income? We determine this by taking your Net (personal) Income and dividing it by your GCI.

_______________ / _______________ = _______________

Net (Personal) Income	GCI	Profit Margin

EXAMPLE: Net (personal) Income $89,700 / GCI $138,000 = 65% Profit margin

If it is difficult for you to fill out your numbers that is probably a good sign that you have identified an area of weakness as a business owner. Remember "Know your numbers!"? It's almost impossible to establish a healthy business without knowing your numbers. So, take this as an opportunity to start getting better.

Let's look at how to use these numbers for your business plan. Here is a really easy way to figure out how much business you need in order to live the life you desire as well as the activity needed to execute.

First, write down *your* desired personal income.

Desired Income: ______________________________

EXAMPLE: $100,000

Now divide *your* desired personal income by *your* profit margin and you'll see exactly how much GCI you need to produce.

____________________ /	____________________ =	____________________
Desired Income	Profit Margin	Required GCI

EXAMPLE: $100,000 / 65% = $153,846.15 Required GCI

Now take your new required GCI and divide it by your average commission and you'll learn exactly how many transactions you need to accomplish your goal.

____________________ /	____________________ =	____________________
Required GCI	Average Commission	Required Annual Transactions

EXAMPLE: $153,846.15 / $7,047 = 21.83 required annual transactions

Now take your annual transactions and divide them by your closing ratio. This calculation will show you exactly how many qualified prospects you need to meet with annually.

____________________ /	____________________ =	____________________
Required Annual Transactions	Closing Ratio Annual Qualified	Prospects

EXAMPLE: 21.83 / 65% = 33.58 annual qualified prospects.

Take your annual qualified prospects and divide it by 48. This represents 48 working weeks in the year. You will take time for family vacations, work trips, holidays, and all kinds of other things that will limit your working capacity. If you know you'll take more time away than that, use the most appropriate number of weeks for your situation. This calculation determines the number of qualified prospects you need to speak with each working week.

________________ / ________________ = ________________

Annual Qualified Prospects	48	Weekly Qualified Prospects

EXAMPLE: 33.58 / 48 = 0.69 weekly qualified prospects

For this person to earn $100,00 of personal income all they need to do is find 0.69 prospects PER WEEK! Anyone can do this. YOU can do this. You can absolutely find one person every week who wants to buy and or sell a house.

Understanding these numbers can catapult business plans that uncover inefficiencies, identify opportunities for improvement and determine core responsibilities that produce your desired results. It's like every business has a hinge pin that everything else relies on. It's that one thing that has to, *has to*, has to get done every day for you to see the results you crave. What is it for you? What is that task that keeps everything together? Is it cold calls? Is it asking for referrals? Is it never missing your coaching calls? What is the glue that holds your business together? Now how often are you pushing that core task aside as if it weren't critical to your success? If I were you, I'd block my calendar off and make it abundantly clear to everyone around that you are not to be disturbed during that time. Everything else must wait. You need to focus so that you all but eliminate the possibility of a bad month or quarter.

6.3. Performance Paradox: When We Look Back to Leap Forward.

To improve your business, taking an honest look, evaluating your past performance, and identifying areas for improvement is wildly helpful. This is not a time to beat yourself up over past mistakes or missed opportunities. Instead, it's an opportunity to learn from your experiences and make changes that will help you achieve your goals. For example, if you spent $10,000 on Facebook ads that only generated 10 leads, that is probably not worth the money. Instead, invest that money somewhere that is generating strong leads, or in an area where you are seeing some level of success. Loyalty to particular marketing plans can be destructive if they don't work. Sometimes things are "just business". You have a responsibility to yourself and those who are relying on you to use each dollar efficiently. These are hard business owner decisions that impact each and every area of your life.

So, take a good, hard look at your past performance and identify what worked, what didn't, and what you can do differently in the future. By doing so, you can create a more effective business plan that considers your past experiences and sets you up for success.

There are a few key levers you can adjust to create the business of your dreams.

We discussed all three of them earlier in this chapter; Average Commission, Closing Ratio and Profit Margin.

Average Commission:

To increase your average commissions, you need to work with a higher price point and/or receive a higher percentage of commission. If you do the same volume of work but with more expensive homes, you will indeed raise your GCI and likely every other positive financial metric. What are three ways you can think of right now to increase your average commission?

Closing Ratio:

What can you do to get 100% of the people you speak with to work with you? How can you be more in demand? How can you present yourself as an expert in your space so that clients are eager to take your input and follow your advice? Do you have a coach? Have you workshopped your listing appointments to death, so you know it backwards and forwards? When I was working at a financial firm, one of the senior advisors promoted what he called "2 AM with a flashlight". The idea was that you needed to know your language and sales pitch so unbelievably well that someone could wake you up at 2AM, put a flashlight in your face and your language is still perfect.

Transitioning from a trusted salesperson to a trusted advisor in someone's life will increase your closing ratios. People love to buy but nobody likes to be sold. Everyone loves an advocate—someone who will look out for you, stand up for you, understand you, and fight on your behalf.

Profit Margin:

There are only two ways to increase a profit margin: increase revenue without increasing expenses or lowering expenses. If you can do both that is a huge win.

Off the top of your head, what are three things you can do this week to increase your revenue? How can you be resourceful and find a way to increase your revenue without incurring additional expenses?

What is your gut reaction when asked "What are three areas you know you can reduce your spending?" Almost every business has some sort of unnecessary spending. What are yours? Identify them and correct them.

6.4. Time to Market: Lights. Camera. Action!

Marketing, growth, and other strategic initiatives are essential to the success of any business, including real estate agents. But these initiatives don't just happen by chance. They require careful planning and execution to be effective.

So, as you create your business plan, be sure to include specific strategies for marketing and growth. This might include things like social media campaigns, networking events, or targeted advertising. Whatever strategies you choose, make sure they align with your overall goals and are measurable so that you can track your progress.

Very few of us can be experts in everything. My overarching opinion is that business owners need to have a working knowledge of every aspect of their business and understand each category in order to make informed decisions. Real estate agents carry many hats and lack the time to become great at all of them. So, in that case, begin to delegate to other professionals who specialize in your industry.

A good marketing plan is measurable. Simply offloading your marketing will not produce the results you desire and is a really good way to throw your hard-earned money down the toilet. Instead, measure it. Track it. Read reports and understand exactly what your money is doing for you so you can decide if you'd like to continue putting money into particular marketing initiatives.

We like to see a 1:10, or 10%, ratio when it comes to marketing and lead generation. That means that every $1 spent needs to produce at least $10 of revenue. If you look at your P&L you can typically show each category as a % of income, so your software does the calculation for you. If you do not yet use a software, you can divide the cost of marketing and lead generation and your GCI.

_______________ / _______________ = _______________

Marketing and Lead Gen Expense	GCI	

EXAMPLE: $12,000 / $96,000 = 12.5%

If your number is above 10%, we would strongly recommend looking into your marketing initiatives and adjust accordingly to get it below 10%. One of the best ways to lower this ratio is to get business from natural markets, introductions and events that cost little to no money.

6.5 SWOT Analysis - self-awareness isn't a commodity

The SWOT analysis is a business tool credited to Albert Humphrey in the 1960s. Albert was a b/usiness consultant, and this exercise is just as effective today as it was back then. SWOT stands for Strengths, Weaknesses, Opportunities, and Threats.

The following is our take on the idea and how it can help you as a part of your business plan. We do this every year for our company and for each individual in our firm, including the owners. It is also what we use for an employee's 90-day review. What we look for in that context is the overall awareness of oneself and a deep understanding of the environment they are in.

Strengths and weaknesses are internal metrics. They are about you and no one else. Opportunities and threats are external or environmental. Likewise, Strengths and opportunities are helpful while weaknesses and threats are hurtful.

Here's what it looks like in a quadrant form:

	HELPFUL	HARMFUL
INTERNAL	**S**TRENGTHS	**W**EAKNESSES
EXTERNAL	**O**PPORTUNITIES	**T**HREATS

Strengths (internal/helpful) - what is it about you that is exceptional? Brag on yourself. What can you hang your hat on knowing you can go up against anyone in your field? What do you do as good or better than anyone else? What part of your personality are you proud of? Maybe you have exceptional patience. Maybe you're a great connector of people. Maybe you're brilliant and you know contract language inside and out. Whatever it is, these are internal things that are helpful for you to obtain your business objectives.

When we do this exercise in our business planning class, I'm always amazed that the strengths list is often the shortest. It can be difficult to perceive yourself in an unapologetically positive light. And yet, you can do it. Be wildly kind to yourself. Work diligently to speak life to your soul and you will build an undeniable wall of certainty that keeps doubts at bay.

Weaknesses (internal/hurtful) - What needs improvement? What parts of your personality and preferences limit your capacity to execute at a high level? What is it about you that limits your success? What part of you has the ability to ruin your business? Weaknesses give us insight into those internal factors that either need attention and improvement or to be hired out. Gary Vaynerchuk is a marketing genius from New York, and he says things like, "double down on your strengths and hire to your weaknesses." I think there's some truth here. However, until you have the ability to hire out, you have to get your weaknesses to a level that they are not catastrophic to your business.

There's an old Jewish proverb that says, "a prudent man sees danger and hides himself but the simple pass on and are punished." Can you see the danger? Do you have the mental fortitude to really look at yourself, see your weaknesses, and adjust appropriately?

One of my (Nathan) greatest weaknesses is that I get bored with projects easily and, oftentimes, flame out on the last 10%. A few years ago, I decided to redo our flooring. I love construction and just building things in general. My first real job was to frame houses in the summer during high school. I really loved that job. It taught me so many things I still use today. Learning how to use tools and build stuff has been super helpful throughout my entire life, especially with three sons who constantly want something built. That said, when I began redoing the floors, I was enthusiastic, inspired, and excited about the quick changes and the much more palatable aesthetics. When I got to the last part of the project, the laundry room, a strange thing happened. While I completed 98% of the floors in two days, there was a small section in the corner of the laundry room that sat unfinished for WEEKS! Why? What the hell am I doing? Why couldn't I just finish the project? Where does that hesitation even come from? From my perspective, the inability to follow something through to its completion is a weakness. I get distracted in the final hour and struggle to keep that energy through the entire project. Part of my struggle is because the project is already completed in my mind, and I've mentally moved on to the next thing. That doesn't eliminate the fact that there's still an entire section of floor mission. So how do you "fix the floor?"

Opportunities (external/helpful) - What are the current and future opportunities for your business, industry, and clients? What is the environment in which you work? What is happening around you that could positively impact your ability to transact at a freakishly high level? Pay attention to the ebb and flow of the market, changing laws and tax codes that you can take advantage of. Research. Learn. Apply. Research. Learn. Apply.

Threats (external/hurtful) - What is happening around you that could negatively impact your ability to execute at a high level? What types of environments hurt the sale of real estate and require a well-thought-out plan to overcome? For example, some agents are currently struggling with extremely low inventory and rising mortgage interest rates. These factors really have nothing to do with agents and can't be solved by an individual agent, but it has everything to do with their business.

Scan the QR CODE below and get your own SWOT analysis. I'd encourage you to take some time to brainstorm each of these categories. Give yourself plenty of time. Take an hour or so. Ponder. Don't just stop at the first initial responses. Instead, make a commitment and dig deeper. One strategy that has worked well for me is to leave the SWOT analysis on my desk for a week or so after my initial brainstorming. Just by seeing it repeatedly, I always find myself adding more things to my lists. The irony is that the most impactful realizations almost always come after my initial brainstorm. There's something about meditating and pondering an idea over and over again that seems to produce abnormally positive results.

Our encouragement is that you take time after reading this chapter to begin answering the following questions. Don't rush. This is your business, and it matters.

Key Questions

1. What would your future self be doing that your present self is not doing?

2. Is your business plan a good business plan?

3. Do you know your numbers or have you exposed a weakness in your business?

Action Steps:

1. Create a clear vision of your future self and what you want to achieve in the coming year. Use this vision to create a roadmap for your business plan.

2. Set measurable and achievable financial goals and objectives for the year ahead, using data from previous years to inform your decisions. Ensure that your goals

are challenging but realistic, and that your business plan has core objectives, goals, systems, and methodologies to accomplish and execute those goals.

3. Monitor your progress regularly and adjust your plans as needed. Identify areas for improvement and make changes that will help you achieve your goals. Be flexible and adaptable to changing market conditions and continue to aim for the target even if you miss the mark sometimes.

Chapter 7

Income Protection - What's the point of making a million dollars if it can be gone in a day?

"There are risks and costs to a program of action. But they are far less than the long-range risks and costs of comfortable inaction."

John Fitzgerald Kennedy

7.1 If there's a hole in the roof, you might want to fix it.

We protect the things we love. We go above and beyond to insulate the people and things we care about from excessive harm and pain. Some do this more instinctively than others, but we all do it. Everyone has a threshold that, when crossed, pushes them into a protective state. While none of us really debate the value of protecting the things we love, we most certainly debate what all needs to be protected and to what extent.

Our suggestion is that the moment you have a business and an income, you will ideally and perfectly protect them.

The loss of your business and personal income can be a catastrophic blow to your life, and we are here to make sure that never happens.

Insurance is nothing more than risk transfer. If you don't want to be caught holding the proverbial bag when your $500,000 house goes up in flames, then you should purchase insurance on your home. Instead of being responsible for the financial pressure of rebuilding your home, you can transfer your financial risk of ruin and rebuild to the insurance company for, fingers crossed, a nominal premium. Simply put, insurance can transfer financial risk from the individual to the insurance company.

Most people buy insurance policies for a few reasons: the government made you buy it, someone sold it to you, or you sought it out because you no longer want to bear the risk of a financial loss. On the other side, the insurer bets that the loss, like your house burning down, will not occur during the policy period. That is the game. The insurance companies win a lot and lose some. And for those who had optimal protection and the insurance did its job, those companies made out like a bank robber—a perfect and complete replacement of the lost asset.

Back when we were working at a financial firm, we were taught that the greatest financial threat we all face is the permanent loss of income. For the vast majority of us, that is true. There are only a couple of people and groups we don't see fitting in this statement. (Taking my liberties, we disregard the uber-wealthy and those in the last stages of life. I only think that because I overthink everything to a fault. There's probably no value in that little caveat but you see how insane I am. So, there's that.)

If you think about it, everything in your financial life is tied to your ability to generate income in one way or another. What would your life be without income? What would change? Could you make it? Could you do all the things you currently do for as long as you would like to do them? If so, you're probably in one of the two groups we mentioned before. For everyone else, without the inflow of money, bills can start piling up and valuable resources are diverting and depleting. That's not exactly a winning combination.

When we work with our financial consulting clients, we always create a personal balance sheet for them. When we discuss this document, we often ask clients, "which of these financial categories is the most important?" We often hear answers like "our real estate," "My retirement account," "my business," and/or whichever category has the biggest number. And while those answers and numbers always have merit, there is only one of a few ways any of these numbers even come to be.

Most assets and liabilities exist because a person generated income and began using it. No matter if they spent it, saved it, invested it, leveraged it, or gave it away, they did something with it and those decisions created the financial environment they are in today. Therefore, income is the cornerstone of a balance sheet. Keep in mind that just because someone has a healthy income does not mean they have a healthy balance sheet. We've seen financial messes with an income that would make you perk up. What we're saying is that without income there's no balance sheet in the first place. Once a client drills down a few logical layers, they begin to realize that everything on their balance sheet is a result of their ability to generate income.

A balance sheet is a snapshot in time. It is the culmination of every financial decision someone has made from the first time their grandma gave them a dollar for their birthday to their current financial landscape. It's a bit intimidating to have all your finances laid out like that. And yet, it is that level of transparency that will provide the foundation for world-class habits and optimal financial decision-making.

So, the question is paramount: what would you do without income?

We are going to discuss three ways agents can protect their income; legal protections, disability insurance and life insurance.

Legal protections can safeguard you in case of lawsuits, errors, omissions, or other liabilities.

Disability insurance helps solve this problem by providing income if you cannot work due to sickness or injury. These payments replace a portion of your lost income for a predetermined amount of time or until you are back at work at your full capacity.

Life insurance is like Plan 1B if disability insurance is 1A. Life insurance is absolutely an income protection tool and should be implemented as such. Life insurance replaces lost income for the deceased and, in some cases, can provide living benefits as well.

7.2. Mike Ross and Harvey Specter. At your service.

It's clearly important to protect yourself and your business from potential liabilities. I mean, no one wants to lose everything they've built. That's just stupid. Here are some key legal considerations and protections to keep in mind:

Entity Selection

The way you set up your business can have a significant impact on whether you are properly protected or not. Each state is different in how it views entities like an LLC. Remember that great deal for California residents? The one where the state does not recognize an LLC as a legitimate business entity for real estate agents. Isn't that fun? An entity that is provided by the IRS is not allowed by the state. HA! Talk about one arm fighting against the other. So that's a big deal.

For Arizona agents, they have to use a PLLC which stands for Professional Limited Liability Company and it must be in the name of the agent. Any mistakes here and the entity, while legal, may not provide any real legal protection.

So, it's not just about getting an LLC and calling it a day. A sound decision requires a working understanding of how states recognize each entity and for whom they are appropriate.

Scan the QR Code below to see your
Secretary of State's Website:

Buy/sell agreements:

If you have multiple business partners, a buy/sell agreement can establish a process for decision-making in case a triggering event occurs. These triggering events, such as death or disability, require one side to buy and one side to sell their shares of the business. It's basically a prenup for your business. A good buy/sell agreement ensures that each member has a way of being made whole amid a triggering event. For Mike and me, we have a robust buy/sell agreement.

When one of us dies, our respective shares go to our estate, as they should. However, if I pass away prematurely, I'm 1,000% sure Mike does not want to be in business with my kids. At least not yet. So, there are two problems. 1.) My kids do not provide the same value to the business that I do but I still want them to receive the full value of what I've built and 2.) Mike needs to legally gain control of the company so he can make decisions moving forward with financial autonomy. The solution is a combination of a buy/sell agreement and life insurance.

When I pass away, Mike is required to buy my shares, and my estate is required to sell my shares. The business owns life insurance for both of us. At death, the life insurance company will send the death benefit to the business (keep in mind that the death benefit from life insurance is income tax free). Mike can then use that money to buy out my kids; producing a clean and easy transfer of ownership where all parties are made whole. We even predetermined the valuation formula in the buy/sell agreement so there is very little to discuss.

If you are in a multi-owner situation, we would strongly recommend addressing these issues before they start. I remember working with a client back at the financial firm. When the owner of this company passed away, they had no legal documents and no life insurance. The owners' kids, who had no role in the business, were now the owners while the key manager, and rightful recipient of the business, ran the company thereafter. The problems started in probate where the kids refused to sell the company and settle their dad's estate. They didn't want to sell because the business was in the midst of a major growth phase and the business was becoming more valuable by the day. The result was that it cost the key manager $3,000,000 more than it should have to buy out the kids because no protections were in place. What went well for the kids, went bad for the business. Not exactly a win-win.

7.3. Disability insurance: the worst named, best insurance

As a business owner, you probably love nothing more than planning for worst-case scenarios, right? There are very few things that really get your weekend going than painstakingly analyzing every way you can financially fail. I mean it really puts you in that peak state ready to conquer the world.

Of course, that's all BS. No one likes to plan for every possible eerie mishap except actuaries. And they're not exactly becoming real estate agents any time soon. So, when we think about the greatest financial threat we all face is the permanent loss of income, there is one type of insurance that directly solves the problem: disability insurance.

While this portion of the book might seem tedious, we want to challenge you to dig deep and go beyond your previous understanding and learn something new. This matters. We recently had a client, who is an agent, make a disability insurance claim and her only regret was not buying more. No joke. She's over the moon and grateful to have her income coming in even though she is working far below normal capacity.

Ok. Here we go. Let's break it down.

Disability insurance has two main types: short-term & long-term. There are consistent components to all disability insurance policies that will be helpful to understand as you make your decision:

Waiting period: How long from an event/diagnosis does someone have to wait before receiving income replacement, aka paychecks.

Benefit period: How long the insurance company will pay you.

Benefit: How much money the insurance company agrees to pay in the case of a claim.

Occupation class: Categorizes an occupation in relation to how much risk or hazard is associated with it. A firefighter would be a more hazardous occupation than a CPA.

Short-Term Disability Insurance:

Short-term disability insurance provides income replacement for, you guessed it, a short amount of time. The waiting period for a short-term disability policy is typically 0-14 days. The benefit period of a short-term disability policy is typically 90 days - one year. These policies cover a small amount of risk. Most of our clients don't continue to buy short-term disability insurance. Instead, we teach clients to cover the financial risk of the first 90-180 days of a disability with savings. While you're in the beginning of a wealth-building phase there is typically not enough savings to safely cover the expense of lost income. In that case, buy it. Buy as much as they will give you.

Long-Term Disability Insurance

It is the "permanent" loss of income that is the major risk, not six months of lost income. Therefore, long-term disability insurance is a major priority and the direct answer to the income-loss problem. There are only a few ways we know to adequately describe how long-term disability insurance works. Our favorite strategy is to look at two jobs: Job A and Job B

Job A vs. Job B

Let's pretend that these two jobs are identical in every way but one. It's the same quality of work. Same quality boss and drive time. They have equal benefits and culture. The ONLY difference is that Job A has offered you $100,000 a year and Job B has offered you $97,000.

JOB A	JOB B
$100,000	$97,000

This isn't a trick question, given the fact that these jobs are identical other than the income, which one does everyone pick? JOB A. No brainer.

Now let's add to it. Let's say that you get sick and can no longer work. JOB A loves you and says, "hey, we love you and would love you to come back as soon as you can. However, since you've been gone for 90 days and you're not working with us anymore, we can no longer pay you. You will always have a place here when you get better." These are nice words and, to be fair, completely reasonable.

Move forward to JOB B. You're in the same situation while employed with JOB B and their offer is radically different. Instead of hearing, "hey, you're not with us anymore so we can't pay you..." you get the following response:

"Thank you so much for all your hard work. Because we value you so much and you're going through such a difficult time we want to make sure you have everything you need. So instead of taking you off payroll, we will continue to pay you $65,000/yr until you get better, or you are 67 years old, whichever happens first. And since things get more expensive, we will actually increase your salary by 3% every year to accommodate. Lastly, if you get better and ever get sick again, we will give you the same deal. You're always welcome here."

JOB A		JOB B
$100,000		$97,000
	After 90 days...	
$0		$65,000/yr
		3% increase every year
		Paid to age 67

Would the response from company B change your mind at all? It would for me! But why would it change your mind? Seriously, tell yourself what it is and think through this. Remember I challenged you to go deeper? Here is your chance. What is the impact of a 3% reduction of your income if you keep receiving paychecks that closely reflect your after-tax income in the case of a sickness or injury? Doesn't that seem like a no-brainer?

Most individual long term disability insurance policies premium is 1%-5% of your gross taxable income. Since most people don't want to add another bill, they refuse to implement good planning and inadvertently expose themselves to the possibility of financial failure. However, imagine if you just started this way. Imagine protecting your income FIRST. Imagine not calculating the insurance cost into your income in the first place and viewing it as Job B with better benefits. If you do not own LTD insurance or know you don't own enough LTD insurance, you can begin that process immediately. You can always reach out to us here at NW Premier or call your life and disability insurance agent.

This next section is in the weeds. It's for all you brainiacs who just have to know more. We'll give you a chance to bail right now and just turn the page. This part isn't critical to your business success but is here for your educational benefit if you want it.

But we are warning you, it is rather tedious.

Still interested? Continue reading and jump back in below.

There are several personal factors and policy designs that impact the premium of policies.

For example: if you bought an insurance policy that had a two-year waiting period and only a five-year benefit period, does the insurance company have a significant risk? NO! Of course not. Most things that could keep you from working won't last two years. Besides, only five years of paychecks is nothing for these companies. The risk is low and therefore the premium is low.

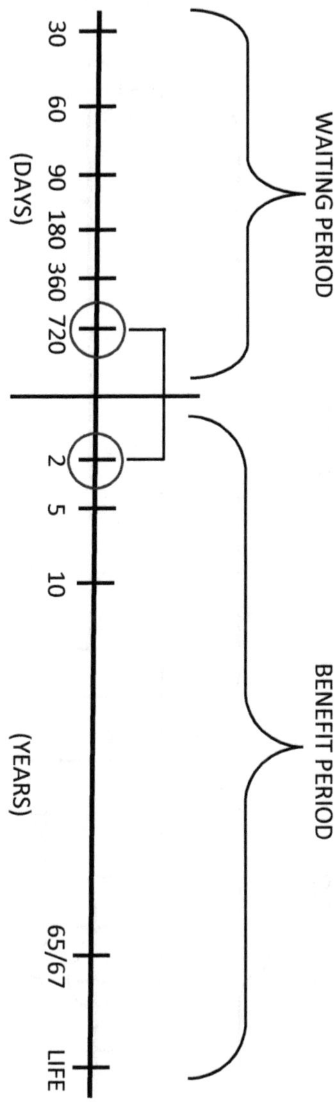

In contrast, if I wanted a 90-day waiting period and wanted income for the rest of my life, the insurance company has significant risk. Potentially millions of dollars. In that case, the insurance company charges a higher premium.

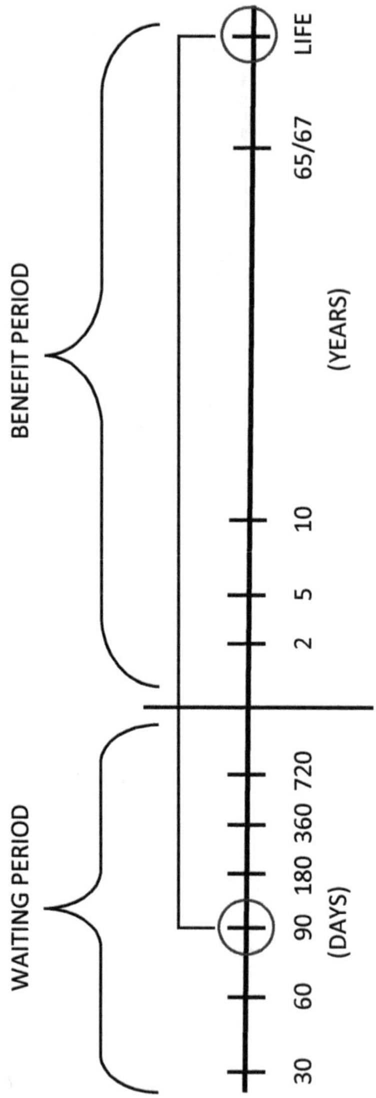

The contract language in these policies can vary significantly. Just because something is labeled as "disability insurance" does not mean they cover the same thing. There are major differences between how these companies define a disability as well. Some say you're disabled if you cannot perform the duties of your job, the one you're educated and trained for. This is called "True Own Occupation". Other policies say you're only disabled if you cannot perform the duties at any job. This is called "Any occupation". Most group policies combine the two. For example, they will allow a True Own Occupation (which is stronger and better) definition for the first two years of the claim and then it switches to Any Occupation. That's fun.

Without boring you with more details and options, the best policies, and the most optimal coverage, are individual policies that have a true own occupation definition, allow for cost of living increases and cover you until retirement or for your entire life.

The key factors that determine your long-term disability insurance payments are your age, sex, and health status. So, if you're a young, healthy woman with a low-risk occupation, congratulations! You're in a low-risk category and your premiums will be lower. But if you're an old, unhealthy male, well, you will probably need to commit more cash flow to get properly protected.

JUMP BACK IN HERE

Whether you select short-term, long-term, or both types of coverage, disability insurance for business owners can provide the peace of mind that your business and livelihood are protected. It can replace a portion of your lost income during periods when you're unable to work and some policies even cover overhead business expenses that continue even when you're disabled.

By planning ahead with the right disability insurance policies, you can help ensure your real estate business continues operating smoothly even if you're sidelined by a sickness or injury. So go ahead, plan for the worst, and hope for the best. It's just good business sense. For a more customized plan talk to your insurance specialist or scan that QR code below and set up an appointment.

7.4. Life Insurance: Protect Your Most Valuable Asset (No, Not Your Yacht)

This has been the hardest section to write. Endlessly staring at an empty page wondering how to even embark on such a vital topic has been paralyzing. Life insurance is a massive topic and, quite honestly, people have intense opinions about it. It's also a subject I know very well. Yet the goal here is to write something of value, not just to wow you with endless knowledge that may or not apply. And that's tough because, from my perspective, it's ALL valuable.

The one message I want to get across is that you should own life insurance. In one way or another, you should use it. Every person I have ever worked with can use life insurance for their benefit. I hate when I hear licensed professionals discuss someone's NEED for life insurance. It's even worse when someone who doesn't understand life insurance says the same thing. There may not always be a need but there is always a purpose. From our perspective, purpose trumps need all day long.

Needs-based planners inadequately convey the value of life insurance and hamstring people with insufficient coverage. There is an amount that is right for you and it's usually close to the IRS limits. That's right. You can't just buy as much life insurance as you want. The IRS has guidelines to determine how much coverage a person can qualify for. Underwriters at these insurance companies approve their policies and stay in compliance to make sure they don't over-insure their applicants. Over insurance is a form of insurance fraud and these enormous companies are not looking to get fined because you want extra coverage.

A great question to ask a life insurance agent is "What is the most coverage I can get?" Just see how they respond. If they balk at this question or just don't know, there's a good chance they don't understand how to properly use the product. If they do calculations about how much debt you have and how much savings you have to calculate your "need" for life insurance, find someone else. These practices hurt people by willfully choosing to quasi-protect their families. They should always be protecting income, not whatever their fancy needs-based calculator tells them. Besides, one of my major qualms with this calculation is the moment you have any change in your financial situation, you have the wrong amount of coverage according to their calculator. Would you really want a coverage amount that could be "off" the moment you make a mortgage payment? Sounds foolish to us. Instead, view life insurance as the ultimate income protection.

The purpose of life insurance, at its core, is income protection. When we think of someone passing away, we don't often think about the loss of income. Hopefully, we're thinking about the more important things like the memories and moments that make that person so special to us. And yet the reality is that there is a financial loss. If there wasn't, a life insurance policy wouldn't even be issued. That's how it works. You must have an insurable interest and that interest is income.

In general, coverage limits are a calculation of income and age.

Age	Coverage limits
18-39	30 x Income
40-49	20 x Income
50-59	15 x Income
60-69	10 x Income
70+	1 x Income or Net Worth (whichever is higher)

The IRS uses a term that we abhor. The language used to determine a person's coverage limit is their "Human Life Value". While no one can determine the value of a life they can certainly determine someone's current economic value, which is what they are really trying to say, as awful as that term may be. Life insurance companies calculate the net present value of future earnings. That is the proper coverage calculation at play.

Think about it in terms of your house burning down like before. If you have a house worth $500,000, would you be ecstatic if your insurance company said, "we know your house is worth $500,000, but do you really NEED a $500,000 house? We think you'd be better off with a $350,00 house. That's enough for you." How would you react? Would you be upset or content? I'd be furious! I want the full replacement value of my home, not a partial replacement. And yet, people choose to only partially protect their income all the time, which is insane because income is ridiculously more valuable than a house. Why would you ever accept less than full replacement value of an asset? And considering that your ability to generate income is your greatest asset, full life insurance coverage is critical to optimal protection planning.

Okay. We've gone super nerdy here. So, let's take a breather and assess. How does knowing the proper coverage limits impact your life insurance decision? Are you even close to right? Do you have any at all? Are you able to close the gap between your current coverage and full replacement?

As we have discussed at length in this book, protecting your income should be the first thing you do with your income. Protection comes first. Think about it, what good is it to build income and wealth if it could all just be gone in a day? Doesn't that feel a bit juvenile?

Protection comes first. That we agree on. The second consideration we have discussed is that protection should be full protection. Full replacement value is what optimal protection looks like.

The last real variable in making your life insurance decision is how long you want the coverage for. This is where a lot of opinions collide. I think our friend Rave Damsey has something to say about it.

There are two major groups when it comes to duration of coverage: term and permanent. Each group has thousands of plan designs to customize policies to your situation. Each group has immense value and a purpose. We are not going to get into the nitty gritty details but we did think it would be valuable for you to understand the key concepts so you can make a good decision for your family.

No matter which type of policy interests you, the key factors that impact your approval rating and consequently your premium remain the same. An approval rating is a result of all the information you provide on an application such as your age, sex, health, smoking habits, personal and family medical history, and more. An applicant with below-average health will receive a low health rating and be much more expensive than the same candidate in excellent health. Smoking has a significant impact on premiums. The simple fact that a candidate smokes often triggers an automatic 25% increase before any other factors are considered. Just right off the bat.

To better understand the differences between term and permanent life insurance, let's discuss three distinguishing categories: length of coverage, cost and living benefits.

TERM:

Length of Coverage:

Term insurance is pure insurance. You pay a premium and they provide the coverage. It is a simple exchange. There's not much else to it. The policy is purchased for a specific amount of time, often five years, 10 years, 20 years or 30 years. Most term policies have a minimum duration of one year and they max out at 30 years.

If someone purchases a 20-year term policy, what do you think happens to the policy the day after the term expires? That's right. It goes away and coverage stops immediately.

It is widely noted that 99% of term policies never pay a death claim. And this is exactly what the insurance companies really want. They want the premium paid and the coverage unused. Think about it like your car insurance. Use it or lose it.

The most common form of term insurance is level term insurance. That means that the death benefit and the premium are guaranteed to not change for the entire term. You keep paying the insurance company $75/mo and they'll keep covering you for $1,000,000. This is wonderfully helpful as you do your financial and protection planning because it eliminates variables, creating predictability and stability.

Cost:

Since 99% of term policies never pay a death claim, do you think the insurance company needs to charge a lot or a little to provide the coverage? If you said "a little" you would be correct. The risk of a death claim is spread out amongst millions of people and therefore the individual gets the price break. Each insured customer enters a collective risk pool that keeps the cost of term insurance reasonably low.

Now, let's pretend there is a 30-year-old, healthy male who purchases a 20-year term policy. The insurance company loves this business because there is a microscopic chance that this individual will die during the contract term. Now let's pretend he is 49 years old and going to outlive his coverage and he wants to extend his coverage. What are his options?

First and foremost, in most cases, to extend coverage our character must be able to medically qualify. But now it's 20 years later. Life has a way of life-ing and he's not in the shape he once was. So now he's 20 years older and in worse health than before. If he can even medically qualify, what do you think happens to the premiums? It skyrockets!

A 50-year-old male with average health purchasing a new 20-year term policy will have a radically higher premium than his previous policy. And this totally makes sense. The possibility of someone dying between 50-70 is significantly higher than 30-50. And this is the game the insurance company is happy to play.

Because premiums rise significantly later in life, term insurance is a save now, pay later type of strategy.

The impact for the 1% of paid claims, however, cannot be overlooked. My very first death claim was a term insurance policy. My client, who had coverage with me for a few years, was killed at work. It was absolutely tragic. His wife and kids were left behind to pick up the pieces. Shattered, the community rallied, and the support was palpable. And yet there was absolutely nothing like letting his family know "You've got $1.5M coming to you right away." I could hear breath enter the atmosphere. A sigh of relief that rivaled all previous sighs.

You could feel peace entering their home knowing they can take as much time as they need to be a family and heal. This moment impacted me forever and I made a commitment to myself to never be shy about advocating the value of life insurance as long as I live.

Living benefits:

There are little to no living benefits with term insurance. Most policies provide some sort of terminal illness rider. This option allows someone to access their death benefit before they die if they are diagnosed with a qualifying serious illness.

This can be incredibly impactful as the end of life with a terminal illness can be painfully expensive.

Some policies will return some of your premium at the end of the policy term for a monthly fee. I usually avoid these as they are abnormally expensive for the benefit they provide.

Term insurance is a wonderful, cost-effective way to get full replacement coverage. If you have never shopped for it, Forbes Advisor reported, "more than half of consumers think the cost of coverage is three times more than it actually is, with 43% of millennials estimating it to be six times higher."

So maybe it's more affordable than you think! If you implement anything from this section, please protect your income. Buy life insurance. Buy as much as you can. Put your money where your mouth is. I've said for years that you can always know a person's priorities by their calendar and their checkbook. People can say whatever they want but numbers don't lie.

PERMANENT:

Length of Coverage:

Permanent life insurance (also known as cash-value life insurance) is exactly what it sounds like. These policies are designed to be permanently in force until the day we all pass away. I mean, if you think about it, when do you really want your life insurance in force? When you die, right? That way you know that you know that you know your life insurance will pay out. And still, as you might expect, not all permanent policies pay a death claim.

Permanent policies have a higher lapse rate, meaning they are no longer in force, in the first one-three years. Having implemented millions in life insurance coverage, I can say that one of my biggest frustrations with permanent life insurance is that it is sold as a silver bullet that fixes all your financial problems in one magical product. And that's a bunch of bullshit. There is no silver financial bullet. So, when people get oversold and then they have concerns or cash flow issues what do you think they do? They bail. They don't understand why they purchased it in the first place and now they are on edge. And canceling might very well be the best choice for them. It completely depends on the totality of the situation. That said, permanent life insurance is not for everyone. Purchasing a policy is a commitment and your decision must be made with that in mind.

These products are very powerful, and that power goes two ways. They can be used to radically improve a person's financial stability or hamstring them with burdensome premiums. I certainly do not want to dissuade you from permanent coverage. Not at all. I love these policies and have implemented them time and time again. I'm simply saying that they must be implemented strategically and appropriately to provide the best benefits possible.

Cost:

The cash flow required to support a cash-value life insurance policy is typically much more than term insurance. This fact can scare several people from implementing it as a part of their protection plan. In fact, some talking heads have suggested that if you just buy term insurance and invest the difference of what you would have paid for a cash value policy, you'll be in a better financial spot. The problem is that they are comparing two completely different financial products and strategies that are really designed to work together not against each other. It should never be an either-or but both and. The invest the difference strategy increases the risk of financial failure, limits retirement income options, and increases tax exposure at death which we are desperately trying to avoid.

One way to explain the big difference between term and permanent is the concept of ownership. The term is a lot like renting. You may have a great place to stay but your rent will never end up back in your pocket. No, your landlord will be happy to cash your checks for the next 20 years while you pay down their mortgage. Wouldn't you?

Permanent life insurance is much more like owning. While the cash required to buy a home is often more than what is required to enter into a rental agreement, the rent payments are gone forever while the mortgage payments are captured by reducing debt and increasing equity. The benefits of homeownership come at a cost. However, I don't think any of the agents reading this book recommend renting over buying. Why? Think of all the reasons you can explain the benefits of owning over renting and you'll understand how I feel about permanent life insurance. That said, there is a time for everything and both types have their much-needed place in our lives.

Think through the logical conclusion regarding cost. It's no secret that contributions to permanent life insurance are higher than the cost of term insurance premiums. However, if you never recapture your premiums paid to the insurance company that shit is expensive. It's a total loss. If you know that one day, one way or another, you'll get all your money back plus some, the only cost is what else you could have done with that money if you implemented a different strategy.

As premiums are contributed to a permanent life insurance policy some of that money is going to the cost of insurance, the commissions to your life insurance agent, policy fees and cash value. Over time the amount of your premium that goes to each place changes, just like a mortgage. As the mortgage matures, more money is spent on principle vs. interest. Similarly, as a life insurance policy matures, more and more of the premium is credited towards cash value. Healthy cash value policies reach a point where each premium paid results in a dollar-for-dollar or better increase in cash value. It basically starts functioning like a high-quality savings account. At some point, usually within the first seven-15 years, the interest on the cash-value account is higher than the premiums required. At that point, the policyholder can begin paying the premium out of interest instead of their cash flow. This allows the insured to pick and choose if and when they'd like to keep paying the premiums out of pocket.

In contrast, term insurance is a save now, pay later strategy while permanent insurance is a pay now, save later strategy.

Living Benefits:

Permanent policies have the same terminal illness options as term insurance, which is just as helpful as before. Many companies provide these features for free which I really appreciate. This option is just so important for families facing tragedy.

Cash-value is a key component of permanent life insurance. Each company has a different method of calculating how cash value gets credited to a policyholder. Some follow an investment index like the S&P 500. Some policies have more specific investment options like stocks and bonds while others distribute cash value from their company's stock and some from a company's dividend. Knowing how your policy creates cash value is helpful in determining which policy is best for you. Each policy design has a different level of risk and may require a different level of investing prowess.

The cash value component to permanent life insurance might be one of the most important and misunderstood benefits of any financial product. That puts permanent insurance to a disadvantage since we tend to fear what we don't understand. So I'll try to make this as plain as I can be so you can make an excellent decision for you and your family.

Cash-value is cash. It is yours. You can use it for whatever you like. It is safe. It is liquid. And it is awesome.

Imagine that a policyholder has $500,000 in their cash value. They are presented with an incredible opportunity to invest in a real estate deal and need $400,000 quickly. Instead of going to get a traditional loan, they think "Hey! What about my cash value? Can I use it for real estate?" The answer is YES. It is your money, and you can use it however you like.

So, if I borrow $400,000 from my account, how much is left? $100,00??? Wrong! This is where the beauty of these policy designs is uncovered.

When you borrow money from your life insurance policy that money does not actually leave your account. Instead, the company secures a loan from their general account against your cash-value. They are insuring the loan with their own product. It's brilliant. They have it covered from all angles. The other protection piece they implement is that they become the primary beneficiary of your life insurance. That way, if you die with a loan outstanding, they receive their money first and any remaining benefit goes to your beneficiaries.

Life Insurance Coverage: $2,500,000
Outstanding Loan: $400,000
Remaining Benefit: $2,100,000

This is how a dollar can be leveraged to do the job of many dollars. This dollar provides a life insurance benefit, receiving interest as cash value, creating interest as a loan and it is also in your real estate investment earning a multiple. That's one dollar doing the job of at least four dollars. The craziest part is that you can't get taxed on the $400,000 because it's not even income, it's a loan. Once the real estate transaction is complete you simply repay the $400,000 and keep the profits. You did all of this with other people's money, you're basically printing money and you're the smartest one at the table.

Be honest, as a responsible adult, you've probably given some thought to what would happen financially if you were suddenly out of the picture. It's a sober reminder that we won't be here forever and the legacy we leave or don't leave, matters. All of this effort you're exhausting to build a business is probably not to bolster your own ego. No, most successful entrepreneurs don't get where they are by pure greed. While that can be an easy narrative to fall into, that has not been my experience. Most successful people have a "why" that is outwardly focused and are some of the most generous people I have ever met. So be consistent. I encourage you to be generous in your protection planning as well. I have never heard someone complain they got too much life insurance when a death benefit was paid. Not a single person has given money back saying it was more than they needed. If you were in that situation, what do you think you'd say? Would you be bummed you got too much or too little? I'm telling you that the reality of the situation is that families always wished they bought more.

Random Thoughts (reader beware)

We are definitely going to get into the weeds of this next part, simply because I love it and that's how my insane brain works. In all honesty, you're welcome to skip ahead if you'd like to avoid my neurotic ramblings. Seriously. I'm not kidding. You might just want to turn the page right now. It won't hurt my feelings.

I'll wait......

Ok. Here we go.

Universal Life and Whole Life are two major types of permanent life insurance. While there are several differences, and you can watch passionate debaters online, we will address a couple differentiators that impact your decision the most. One of the most important distinctions is how they calculate the cost of insurance.

Universal life policies unbundle their contract and recalculate the cost of insurance each year. This can be exceptional for younger insureds as the cost of insurance is typically lowest when you're younger. The lower cost of insurance gives the policy time to perform, increasing its cash value to support the rising costs of insurance in later years. The goal is for the policy's cash value to outpace the cost of insurance.

If insurance is less expensive in the early years, the opposite is also true, the cost is highest when you're oldest. Universal life policies bank on the idea that the policy will perform at a predictably high level so there is a very limited exposure in older years. If the policy does not perform at its predicted rate, additional premiums may be required to keep the policy in force. If the policy does perform as expected, there is a strong likelihood it will in fact be in force at death.

Whole life insurance is designed the exact opposite way. They bundle all the costs by calculating total life expectancy and averaging the cost of insurance to provide a guaranteed level premium for the life of the contract, just like the level term. The early years of a whole life policy require more cash flow than a universal life policy. However, as the insured gets older, the cost of insurance does not increase at all. It cannot. It is already levelized. This is a huge advantage as no additional premiums can be required to keep a policy in force in later years. While guarantees can be expensive, losing coverage in the 11th hour is arguably more problematic.

In universal life policies, the cash value is subject to a surrender period where not all your cash is immediately available. Whole life policies do not have a surrender period meaning whatever money is in the cash value account is available for you to use at any time and reason.

To access the cash value, you simply contact your life insurance company and request it. You can either pull the money out as cash or borrow it from yourself, paying yourself interest. Leveraging your cash value can be an excellent way to build wealth.

As a general rule, we prefer whole life because the death benefit and premium are guaranteed, the cash-value is way more predictable and the policy is more flexible. The premium is guaranteed to never increase and the death benefit is guaranteed to never go down. In fact, not only does the death benefit not go down, but many whole-life policies have an INCREASING death benefit. I love this feature because if I purchase $1,000,000 of coverage today, that death benefit does not have nearly the same value 30 years from now. Things get more expensive and the dollar becomes less valuable. That little situation is called inflation. And I still want my death benefit to feel as much like $1,000,000 as it can, even in 30 years. An increasing death benefit allows for this and gives the policyholder more flexibility with contributions made directly to cash value.

7.5. It's not exactly set it and forget it

As your business grows and you start making more money, it's important to remember that your protection needs to grow too. After all, the permanent loss of income is the greatest financial threat we all face. That's why it's beneficial to have a protection-first philosophy and make sure your income is going to come in regardless of what happens - whether it's death, disability, or any other unexpected event.

When you think of your most ambitious goals, how many things have to go right for them to work out? Would it be fair to say that basically everything has to go right? I think so. Analyze the other side of that equation. How many things would have to go wrong for it to be dramatically different? The truth is, it only takes one major event to disrupt your income stream and leave you and your loved ones in financial trouble. That's why it's so important to regularly check in on your insurance and legal policies to ensure that you're well-protected.

Make it a point to have a once-a-year check-in with all your policies to ensure that they're still meeting your objectives. As your income and business grow, you may need to adjust your policies to make sure that you're still optimally covered. Don't assume that your current policies will still be sufficient in the future - take the time to review them regularly to ensure that you're prepared for any eventuality.

At the end of the day, your responsibility is to make sure that your income is protected, no matter what happens. By taking a proactive approach to your insurance and legal policies, you can ensure that your business and your loved ones are always well-protected.

Key Questions:

1. What's something you love that you have yet to protect?

2. What does optimal income protection look like for you?

3. What adjustments would you make in your protection if money wasn't a factor?

Action Steps:

1. Evaluate what income protection policies you currently have in place and determine if additional coverage is needed.

2. Work with a lawyer to address any legal protection concerns.

3. Schedule time each year to ensure coverage amounts are still sufficient, make any necessary changes, and determine if additional policies should be added based on your current income and business situation.

Chapter 8

Using Debt to Build Wealth - Wait. What?

"Debt is a good servant but a bad master."
Sir Francis Bacon

8.1. Debt - an unlikely best friend

Some personal finance gurus would say, avoid all debt like the plague (*Cough Cough* Some guy named Rave Damsey *Cough Cough*), but let's face it - entrepreneurs think differently. What works for the average person just doesn't apply when you're building wealth through business ownership.

One of our favorite wealth building strategies for entrepreneurs is the "OPM Plan" which stands for Other People's Money. Business debt can be a real game-changer for your real estate business. Business loans give you the power to launch or expand your operations and purchase assets that generate income. One of the incredible things about borrowing debt is that it is not income so there are no income taxes associated with receiving the loan. Good business debt, used strategically, can supercharge growth and returns on investment.

Business debt can come in handy for several purposes such as covering startup costs, funding operating expenses, making investments that generate income, and managing cyclical cash flow with lines of credit. However, taking on business loans requires confidence, a solid business plan, and discipline. Before you dive in, model your cash flow and revenue projections, have a clear growth strategy, and plan for contingencies in case your projections fall short. A good debt strategy will always include a "worst-case scenario" that should still provide a way to service the debt. That said, as entrepreneurs, we are all mostly optimistic and never think about failing. It's a tough conversation but it needs to happen. We say, rip off the Band-Aid, have the conversation, address it, then stuff it back in the drawer hopefully never to be looked at again.

While business debt can be "scary as f--" at first, capitalizing on the "OPM Plan" through strategic borrowing shows you're willing to take the risks required to succeed as an entrepreneur. Bet on yourself and your abilities - but do it intelligently, with a sound plan for how the debt will drive profit. By using business loans responsibly, you can accelerate the growth of your real estate venture and not dip into your personal bank accounts or other assets.

8.2. Not all debt is created equal

Americans are often taught to avoid debt at all costs and to prioritize paying off any debts they do have as quickly as possible. Couldn't you just imagine credit card companies paying millions of dollars to teach us to pay them back first? It sounds logical, but inappropriately prioritizing paying off debt often leads to a vicious debt cycle.

However, not all debt is created equal. In fact, some types of debt can actually be beneficial when used correctly. Let's take a closer look at the difference between good debt and bad debt.

Good Debt:

Good debt is productive debt. It must be doing something for you. It can be thought of as an investment in your future. This type of debt is usually taken on for a specific purpose, such as purchasing a home, starting or expanding a business, or investing in education. Good debt is ultimately used to fuel an asset that creates a positive return on investment, meaning that the benefits of the debt outweigh the costs over time.

Examples of good debt include:

- Mortgage: A mortgage is considered good debt because it allows you to purchase a home, which can appreciate in value over time. Additionally, the interest on your mortgage may be tax deductible, which can lower your overall tax burden.

- Business loan: Taking out a loan to start or expand a business can be a wise investment in your future earning potential. If you use the loan to grow your business, the increased revenue can more than offset the costs of the loan.

- Personal loan: Sometimes, taking out a personal loan can be a smart move. For example, if you need to consolidate high-interest credit card debt into a lower-interest loan, you could save money on interest charges over time.

- College debt: While many people view student loans as a burden, they can actually be a smart investment in your future earning potential. If you use your education to land a higher-paying job, the benefits of your degree can outweigh the costs of the loan.

Good debt is any debt that is taken on with a plan for how it will help you achieve your financial goals. If you can use the borrowed money to increase your income and net worth over time, it is likely to be a wise investment.

Ultimately this is a balance sheet conversation. The end goal is to build net worth, not to simply reduce debt. We live in a whole new era of how money works. Gone are the times of being able to work your way through college and have no debt. Long gone are the times of employees being able to buy a home with almost any wage at any job. We have to learn new ways of building wealth and looking at money. Debt can be a powerful tool for wealth creation. To be fair, an agent can definitely get over their skis and it can have an opposite effect. Therefore, you should track the impact of debt to ensure you are getting a return that justifies the debt.

For example, if I borrow money at 8%, I have to use that money for something that creates more than an 8% return. If I can accomplish this task, the bet pays off. If not, I lose... big time.

Bad Debt:

Bad debt is unproductive debt. Bad debt is taken on without a clear plan for how it will make you money in the long run. This type of debt is often used for things like vacations, luxury purchases, cars, clothing and other non-essential expenses.

Examples of bad debt include:

- Revolving credit card debt: Credit card debt is often considered bad debt because of the high-interest charges, no amortization and most often it could be avoided with healthy financial habits.

- Car loans: While it's not always the case, car loans are often considered bad debt because cars depreciate in value over time, meaning that you may end up owing more on the car than it is worth. How much you borrow on the vehicle and the interest rate greatly affect which category car loans apply.

- Payday loans: Payday loans are a type of short-term loan that often comes with extremely high interest rates. They are considered bad debt because they can trap borrowers in a cycle of debt that is difficult to escape.

8.3. Annoyingly common debt traps and pitfalls. Watch your step!

As a real estate agent, it's important to be aware of the common debt traps and pitfalls that can derail your financial goals. Here are a couple of common pitfalls to avoid:

1. Magical Investment Opportunities: One common debt trap for real estate agents is investing in marketing companies or other "opportunities" that promise to boost your lead generation and overall business. While some of these opportunities may be legitimate, many are simply ways for companies to take your money without delivering any real value in return. Before investing in any opportunity, be sure to do your due diligence and research the company thoroughly. It is amazing to us how many businesses sell their products and services to new agents with little to no accountability. Ask them what their accountability is in the transaction and how that impacts you if they do not perform. Make sure to read the contract and hold them accountable along the way.

2. Paying off Debt before Building Savings: Let's say you have $20,000 in debt and you make your first sale, earning $10,000. Many people would use that money to pay off their bills and debt first. While it may seem like the responsible thing to do, this approach can actually put you in a precarious financial position. Once you pay your credit card balance, that money is gone forever. You no longer have any say in how it is used and it can no longer be of any future benefit to you. Instead, go back to a balance sheet approach.

You have two main options in this scenario. In the first example we have no money (assets) and $20,000 of debt.

Assets	Liabilities
$0	$20,000
	Net Worth
	($20,000)

If this person makes $10,000, they have two choices of where to put it.

OPTION 1: Reduce Liabilities

Assets	Liabilities
$0	$20,000
	-$10,000
	$10,000
	Net Worth
	($10,000)

You can see that the net worth in OPTION 1 was increased by $10,000 when the debt was reduced by the same amount.

OPTION 2: Increase Assets

Assets	Liabilities
$10,000	$20,000
	Net Worth
	($10,000)

In OPTION 2 we see that the net worth has not changed from option 1. But what, then, is the difference between these two? The biggest differences are interest and control. In OPTION 1 you pay less interest and have zero control over your money. The interest rate you can earn is fixed according to the interest rate of the credit card.

In OPTION 2 you pay more interest on debt and have complete control over your money. You can use the money for investing in your business or other income generating activities. If you can use that money to earn more than the debt is charging you, use it and you win.

There is a third option but it's simply a combination of the two above. This works well when there is excellent and predictable cash flow.

You can also think about it this way; if something goes wrong and you don't have savings (like in OPTION 1), where will you get the money to cover unexpected expenses? If you don't have savings, you may end up going right back into debt. Additionally, if you use all your earnings to pay off debt, you may not have any money left to reinvest in your business or to handle the ups and downs of commission-only income. This can create a cycle of debt that is difficult to escape.

To avoid this pitfall, strike a balance between paying off debt and building up savings. Consider setting aside a portion of your earnings each month for an emergency fund and an opportunity fund. This way, you'll have a safety net in case of unexpected expenses, and you can continue to grow your business over time.

8.4. Keep your eye on the prize

For real estate agents who want to build a strong financial foundation, managing debt effectively and responsibly is completely possible and attainable. Here are a couple of strategies to consider:

We talked about prioritizing putting money into Savings instead of paying it straight towards debt. While it's clearly important to pay off debt, it's also important to build up savings as you can see demonstrated in the tables of the last section of this chapter. Instead of putting all of your extra money towards paying off debt, consider setting aside a portion of your earnings each month that's safe and available. Your savings might come in handy for unseen events happening like your car breaking down or, I don't know, taxes?

Now this input may sound elementary, but remember, you're a business owner now and must act like one. Top producing agents who have made that transition to business owner are acutely aware that they are responsible for setting aside the embedded tax liability in their income. Failure to plan ahead and prepare to pay your taxes can lead to penalties, interest charges, and other financial problems. Nobody wants that. To avoid this pitfall, make sure you are setting aside enough money each month to cover your estimated taxes. Our recommendation is to set aside slightly more than your previous year's tax rate. For example: if last year you paid 28.6% in taxes, save 30% of each commission. A good CPA can also calculate your estimated taxes each quarter and can give you a schedule to follow for on time payments.

By putting money into savings instead of paying it straight towards debt and not forgetting about taxes, you can set yourself up for long-term financial success. Remember, building wealth is a marathon, not a sprint. It's all about having a financial order of operations. By taking a steady and consistent approach to managing your finances, you can achieve your financial goals over time.

8.5. Don't judge a book by its cover - leveraging debt wisely

I think we can all agree that debt can be a powerful tool for real estate agents looking to grow their businesses and create long-term wealth. We thought it would be helpful to give you some ways we have witnessed agents use debt productively. Keep in mind that there are no cookie cutter options here. Trust your gut. Spend money on the things that make sense to you and provide a clear path to profit.

Invest in your number one investment, yourself! You are your business. Anything you can do to enhance your personal development, educate yourself, develop expertise and really look the part will all be wildly beneficial.

For example let's say you are just starting out in the business and are considering investing $10,000 into your image, website and/or marketing. You really have two options.

Option1 - Take from your savings and lower your savings account by $10,000. You don't add additional debt to your balance sheet because you can technically afford everything you'd like to do. This option is obviously riskier if your cash reserves are limited.

Option 2 - You borrow $10,000 from a bank to fund your strategy. This way you don't dip into your savings account, and you now have the additional money at a small monthly payment. In this scenario you are hoping that the borrowed $10,000 will produce way more revenue than it cost to borrow the money. Let's say the average house price in your area is $350,000 and the average commission is 3%. If you sell one home from your investment strategy you are in the money. Rinse and repeat.

Let's take one more example that may or may not be a controversial saying. There is an old movie called *Boiler Room* starring many great actors including Ben Affleck. In one of his speeches to the new interns at his financial advisory firm he tells them all to go buy nice suits and "act as if". When starting a new business, it is important to dress and act the part of a professional for your industry. For many realtors that is a nice outfit, website, headshots, watches, haircut etc. You're investing in your image and as the old saying goes, look good, feel good.

Another boost to your self-image starts in your brain. Growing, learning and eliminating negative talk all bolster your confidence. In order to become the best, you have to be learning from the best. Most of the highest performing realtors we work with invest in business coaches, seminars, training and some sort of education to expand their mind in business. Look into these different ways to invest in yourself and budget them into your business plan for the year. One of the fastest ways to grow your business is to submerge yourself with high performers and learn everything you possibly can from them.

Ultimately, the key to leveraging debt for business growth and wealth creation is to be strategic and mindful about how you use borrowed money. While it can be tempting to take on as much debt as possible, it's important to remember that debt comes with interest charges that add up over time. Be sure to do your due diligence and research your borrowing options carefully before making any decisions.

Key Questions:

1. What types of good debt and bad debt do you currently have?

2. Are you more interested in reducing interest charges or having more control of your money?

3. How can you best plan to use debt productively?

Action Steps:

1. Create a clear plan for how you will use borrowed money to achieve your financial goals. Be sure to differentiate between good debt and bad debt, and only take on debt that will produce a positive return on investment.

2. Build up savings in addition to paying off debt. Consider setting aside a portion of your earnings each month for an emergency fund and business investments.

3. Do your due diligence and research your borrowing options carefully before making any decisions. Consider working with a financial professional to help you navigate the complex world of debt.

Chapter 9

Buying Your Own Product - the cobbler's kids have no shoes

"A good example has twice the value of good advice"
Albert Schweitzer

9.1. It's time to walk the talk

Whenever you go to a networking event, every time, without fail, there will be five real estate agents and six life insurance agents. The life insurance agents are all fishing for whales and the other four real estate agents blunder and say shit like, "I just want to help anyone anywhere buy or sell any home." Puke. The problem in our made up, though very realistic, scenario doesn't end with putrid answers to, "what do you do?" Nope, that's where they start. After a brief discussion, you learn that only two of the six life insurance agents own any life insurance at all. That means four of these life insurance agents have no personal experience with filling out their own application, experiencing underwriting or committing to pay premiums. They can't even explain why someone in their position would own life insurance, but they still want you to buy it from them and send them all your business owner friends. Fat chance.

The two life agents who own their own policies have a massive advantage over the four who do not. They have a personal story, confirmed buy-in and substantiated the authenticity of their business. They speak with authority because they are walking the walk. They are on your side. They are with you. Think about this, if we had never built NW Premier, a business focused on advocating for real estate agents with consistent and massive results, would you even give two shits about the information in this book? Of course not! Our authority comes from a mountain of undeniable evidence that we are who we say we are. And the same is true for you.

Going back to our nearsighted life insurance agents, which agent would you prefer to listen to and buy from: the ones who own life insurance or the ones who do not? And really think about this? What are two or three reasons you can come up that impacted your decision?

When it comes to financial products, most of us are wary of buying something that a salesperson doesn't personally own. After all, why would we trust someone to recommend a product that they won't invest in themselves? Believe it or not, it's the same with real estate!

Real estate agents benefit greatly when they experience what their customers are also experiencing. You can absolutely buy and sell real estate before you own a home, but it would behoove you to make buying a home a massive priority. The way you felt about the life insurance agent who was unprotected is how people feel about hiring real estate agents who don't own their own house. There will always be a sliver of doubt when you recommend, they buy a home or invest in a property if you haven't gone through the process yourself. They'll inevitably wonder across the thought, "it's easy for you to decide what to do with other people's money, isn't it?" And isn't that accurate? Isn't that fair? While you can buy and sell properties without owning your own, not buying your own real estate creates hurdles on your way to success. It limits your authority. It's just how it is.

Let's say that you want to go to a new restaurant and are looking for recommendations. You made a Facebook post and now people are happy to respond. Now imagine you received a recommendation that sounded something like this: "Hey! I heard there was a new place that opened up on Main St. not long ago. My friend went there and said it was good, but I haven't been. I've been thinking about it though."

Now what if that same person wrote this recommendation instead: "Oh my goodness, you have to try that place on Main St. We went there last week and it was incredible. I had the chef's special, and it was to die for. I would totally go with you if you wanted to go."

Which recommendation would have a higher chance of getting you to visit the restaurant?

Not owning your own product is like recommending someone to try a restaurant that you haven't gone to. It's not providing the depth of value and expertise that builds the trust and leadership your customers deserve.

If you want to separate yourself as a real estate agent and provide additional value to your customers, go through the experience yourself and own property. Represent the market you're selling to. If you want to sell to real estate investors, invest in real estate yourself. By doing so, you'll have a better understanding of the market and be able to provide more valuable insights and expertise to your customers. It will also help you transition from a trusted salesperson to a trusted advisor in this person's life. Selling from a place or authority and experience is far more powerful than selling from a place of regurgitated secondhand knowledge.

Not only that, owning real estate demonstrates to your customers that you take your job seriously and are committed to the industry. If you're an agent who doesn't own a home, customers may not take you seriously or trust your recommendations as much. It's an odd thing but it's just true. I would never take investing advice from a financial advisor who doesn't invest their own money. No way. Not a fucking chance.

The further along you are in your real estate journey, the more expertise you'll be able to provide to your customers. Clients will ask you, "what would you do in this situation?" and you can answer from a database of moments and decisions that you experienced yourself. You'll be able to offer valuable insights and advice on the buying and selling process, financing options, and more. In order to stand out in the industry, start by walking the walk and investing in real estate yourself.

9.2. We are not the same: Active income vs. passive income

Have you ever been to an employee store of a major corporation? It is so fun. We live near Nike's world headquarters so, naturally, several people in our community work there. Nike has an incredible employee store and a couple times a year, usually around the start of school and Christmas, someone gives us a pass so we can visit the employee store. Everything in the entire store is at least 40% off from retail. The last time I went I purchased nine pairs of shoes for my family! It felt great to see that 40% off on the receipt. I was so thankful to the person who got me the pass and my kids were ecstatic with their new school shoes. Besides the joy on my kids' faces, my favorite part was the discount. What can I say? I love a good deal.

As a real estate professional, your "employee store" consists of all the real estate in the United States. When real estate professionals own real estate investments, the IRS allows you to classify income in a way that is a colossal advantage over a non-real estate professional, like myself. The IRS treats real estate professionals and non-real estate professionals differently. And since you're going to invest in real estate anyway, let's make sure you understand this income distinction and its tax implications.

First, in order to be recognized as a real estate professional by the IRS, certain criteria must be met. The two criteria are as follows: 1.) More than half of the personal services performed in all trades or businesses during the tax year were performed in real property trades or businesses in which the taxpayer materially participated; and 2.) the taxpayer performed more than 750 hours of services during the tax year in real property trades or businesses in which he or she materially participated (Sec. 469(c)(7)(B)).

If you meet these criteria, the IRS views the income generated from your real estate activities differently than for those who don't. Keep in mind that your license does not qualify you as a real estate professional. If that were the case, there'd be a ton more non-producing agents out there taking advantage of the opportunities below.

There are several types of income according to the IRS. For our conversation let's focus on active income and passive income.

Active income is the income we work for. Maybe you clock in to work or provide a specific service and are then compensated financially; that is active income. Selling a home would fit in this category. It's money you actively work for.

Passive income is unearned income. You didn't have to work for it, or maybe it took minimal effort. It's the kind of income you can make while drinking a Mai Tai on the beach. That's the kind of income Mike loves; one in which he can earn while having a drink with an umbrella in it. In fact, he loves umbrella drinks in general. He says they're good for the soul. Maybe he's onto something there. Back to the idea here, if I own a rental property, I am not actively working to receive that income. No, I simply own the asset and the asset is really the one doing the work here, not me.

A well-known tax principle is that you cannot deduct passive losses against active income. To explain this concept let's say Mike and I own real estate together. We bought a new property this year and took a massive loss. We had all kinds of deductible expenses and only rented the property for the last two months of the year. In this case, for non-real estate professionals, we can reduce the income we received from the property to $0 through calculating expenses but we cannot go below zero. We cannot deduct losses from unearned income against the income we make in our business. It's quite frustrating, but that's how it is. However, for real estate professionals, that rental income that was counted as passive for us has a wonderful metamorphosis and miraculously turns into active income per the IRS.

The ability to deduct losses from rental income against active income is a freaking gamechanger. This strategy can lead to significant tax efficiencies that non-real estate professionals simply do not get.

	Real Estate Professional	Non-Real Estate Professional
Active Income	$200,000	$200,000
Passive Losses	($50,000)	($50,000)
Passive Losses Realized	($50,000)	$0
Total Taxable Income	$150,000	$200,000
Income Taxes @ 35%	$52,500	$70,000

This means that the non-real estate professional has to pay an additional $17,500 in taxes compared to the real estate professional. That's why this is your "company store".

Visualize this opportunity. Think of purchasing property like you're at an employee store with a steep discount. It's insanely powerful. Real estate professionals build wealth with incredible tax efficiency if they understand the fundamentals of income classification. You got this!

9.3. Sometimes the grass is greener due to a septic issue

Remember how frustrated we were with life insurance agents inappropriately selling cash-value policies as if they were a silver bullet? Well, many real estate agents do the same thing. They talk as if you get one rental property and you're set for life. Just have some sort of investment in real estate and you're way ahead of the rest. And that's just not the case. There is power in numbers. Successful investors rent multiple doors and therefore radically limit much of the exposure they have to poor renters, unexpected expenses and adverse market conditions. In fact, two experts we recently spoke with recommend starting with a plan to own at least 10 rentals or to not even start at all. How do you feel about that?

The idea is simple; if you have three rental homes and something happens on one property, 33% of your rental portfolio is at risk. If you have 10 rental homes and something happens on one property, only 10% of your portfolio is at risk. Multiple doors spread the risk of a negative tenant experience or issues with the house.

Have you ever heard of those tenants who totally trash a property, take the blinds, let their kids turn the walls into a crayon cathedral and leave sour milk in the refrigerator after they unplugged and de-iced it all over the kitchen? Yeah. That one. When they inevitably appear, your risk is already diluted with multiple doors. When you have multiple doors to rent, you'll likely have the cash flow and capacity to cover the cleanup on aisle three. If you only had one door, this situation might be a devastating blow.

Oh, and speaking of tenants, it sure feels like most current laws support them instead of the property owner. It's getting more and more difficult in many of America's cities to operate as a landlord without experiencing serious tenant grief. I have heard story after story about tenant and squatter disputes unnecessarily costing investors thousands of dollars. So, if you're a landlord, having a plan for dealing with difficult tenants is standard operating procedure. It sure can be tough to get control of a property when things go wrong. Before all the chaos begins you can eliminate many problems by having a robust application process, excellent rental agreements (written by a real attorney), insurance and significant deposits.

It is clear from this book that we are huge fans of real estate. In all seriousness, investing in real estate properties is one of the best ways to build wealth and financial security. But let's not pretend like it doesn't come without its risks. I personally know people who have gone bankrupt, and it was real estate that sunk them. You know them, too! All that said, regardless of the risks, absolutely go for it. Get all that you desire. Just take the time to ask yourself, "what could go wrong?" Address that nasty stuff before it even happens. You can be an outstanding real estate agent with an outstanding real estate portfolio. You can take advantage of all the incredible tax benefits of being a real estate professional and keep as much money in your business and family as possible.

Key Questions:

1. What can you do to build your expertise and authority?

2. On a scale of 1-10, how important is it for you to buy rental properties?

3. How are you preparing to buy your own product?

Action Steps:

1. Develop a comprehensive plan for investing in real estate that aligns with your financial goals and risk tolerance.

2. Research different types of properties and investment strategies to determine what best fits your investment goals and expertise. Consider factors such as location, property type, rental income potential, and potential for appreciation.

3. Network with other real estate professionals and investors to gain insights and learn about potential investment opportunities. Attend industry events and join local real estate investment groups to expand your network and stay up to date on market trends.

4. Be transparent with your clients about your own real estate investments and experiences. Use your expertise to provide valuable insights to help clients make informed decisions.

Chapter 10

"Help! I need somebody!" - The Beatles

It is literally true that you can succeed best and quickest by helping others to succeed.

Napoleon Hill

When we first started out in financial services, we met with CPAs, bookkeepers, P&C insurance agents, roofers, plumbers, marketing companies, SEO specialists, videographers, photographers—you name it. We wanted to not only build out our team for ourselves but also for when our clients need an introduction. Nothing increases your sway with clients more than having world-class introductions and therefore becoming their trusted advisor. You become their go-to resource no matter what they need. A simple way to enhance your role with your clients is to provide other professional connections that reflect the quality of your business. They win, you win. It's that simple. And the success of their work is automatically credited to you.

Creating a network of help is not overly complicated. Many successful agents started out by relying on their mentors, doing their research, finding the right fit, and sustained it all by cultivating those relationships over time. These connections are for you and your clients. In fact, your support team of professionals will become your secret weapons. They will be providing you with outstanding support allowing you to focus your energy on helping clients.

10.1. From Trusted Salesperson to Trusted Advisor - The Go-to Person.

It's been said time and time again that "it's not what you know, it's who you know." Top producing agents make a beautiful transition from being a trusted salesperson to being a trusted advisor. Much of this happens after building an exceptional network of help. But it never just starts out this way.

Let's face it, at the beginning of your career, you are doing whatever you can to obtain clients, sell homes, pay bills and put food on the table. All of your energy is focused on survival and every business owner has been there! We remember when we were doing everything we could to make payroll AND pay our rent on time in the same month. This is a normal part of the journey, and we respect it.

Over time, you have more wins than losses and you start thinking you might just make this thing work for real. And while you're gaining valuable experience, you are also naturally expanding your network. You begin to work with people enough to know if you can trust them and if they are in alignment with your values.

If you follow our advice and build a network of help for your clients, you will quickly build credibility and become the go to person for your clients when any issues come up even if it doesn't involve real estate. The goal is for them to think about you for everything, not just for real estate.

10.2. Mirror, mirror on the wall...

When you make an introduction, your client will attribute their quality to you. If you just send people to the roofer who is providing you with business but they suck ass at their job, their poor quality will be transposed to you. The opposite is also true. When you introduce a client to an excellent company, it validates their decision to hire you and builds trust at an astonishing rate. Therefore, your focus is to be on the quality of service they provide, not in reciprocating referrals. You are an advocate for your clients. Your job is to protect them and make sure they have the best possible experience. You are not in the business of leveraging your clients to bolster your BNI chapter. Fuck that shit.

You got into this business because you are a wonderful connector of people. And this is no different. Instead of connecting for a sale, you're connecting to improve any possible area of their life. Need an attorney? I got one. Need an insurance agent? No problem. Need a plumber? I've got three. Be the go-to resource for quality introductions and your reputation and efficiency will soar.

Once you've built your team of professionals, it's important to cultivate those relationships over time. Treat them like partners in your success, and be proactive about consistently seeking guidance and advice, not just when things go wrong. Treat these professionals like clients of yours. Add them to your follow up calls, send them holiday or birthday cards and make sure they know you're still there year-round. By building strong relationships with your professional network, you'll be well-positioned to succeed in the world of real estate.

Key Questions

1. Who are the most valuable people you can introduce to your clients?

2. How does receiving a positive referral impact how you view the referrer?

3. Which of your current referral partners are not representing you well?

Action Steps:

1. Reach out to real estate mentors and colleagues for referrals to build your network

2. Ask your clients for feedback as you introduce them to other professionals. Let your clients know if you have had a personal experience with their work or not.

Chapter 11

Social Benefits of Home Ownership - you are ridiculously more important that you realize

If you believe your product or service can fulfill a true need, it's your moral obligation to sell it.

-Eleanor Roosevelt

This section is designed to fire you the fuck up and inspire you to take massive action in order to produce outrageous results. And you won't be doing this all for yourself. Nope! After reading this section, I'd be shocked if you didn't increase your sales and fight like hell for your family and friends too. Without question, real estate agents have a unique opportunity to make a positive impact on people's lives. By helping your clients find their dream home, you're not just selling them a property – you're selling them a better life. Buying a home initiates a beautiful domino effect, positively impacting multiple social categories. It is such a joy when agents understand these impacts. They engage with their businesses with an abnormal fervor and are cemented as mission oriented, passionately advocating for their people.

11.1. You have the power to change the world

We often ask agents, "what do you sell?" It's such a goofy question because it is blatantly obvious that they sell real estate. They're licensed real estate agents, for goodness' sake. And so, they always look at us funny. Yet, the simple fact that we asked the question inherently implies that they do not know the answer we're looking for. So, we let them look at us funny and we ask again, "tell me. What do you sell?" When they answer they always say, "real estate" but the inflection in their tone is more like a question: "real estate?"

Instead of just letting them off the hook we usually respond with, "got it. And what else are you selling?" What we're getting at here is that there are other areas of life that are impacted when owning a home. And some of these impacts affect us and our futures greatly. So, the question becomes, do you intimately know the details and impact of what you sell? Do you understand your product in totality, not just operationally? Do you know the influence that real estate has on things like family health, physical health, mental health, education and financial stability? If you don't, this chapter is for you.

Selling real estate is so much more than just selling the home itself. It becomes what the home represents. It is a deeper conviction that fuels an unending fire to be the best damn agent you can possibly be.

The value of homeownership exceeds having a place to call your own just like being a real estate agent is so much more than just selling houses. Studies have shown that owning a home can lead to increased civic participation, better health outcomes, and improved educational attainment. When you own a home, you have a greater stake in your community, and you're more likely to invest in it. Homeownership creates a sense of pride and belonging, and it fosters a sense of stability that can have a ripple effect throughout the community.

The National Association of Realtors put out an incredible paper in December 2016. This paper titled "Social Benefits of Homeownership and Stable Housing" by Lawrence Yun, Ph. D. and Nadia Evangelou is a freaking goldmine of information and perspective. You can view that paper by scanning this QR code.

This paper offers a plethora of research and statistics that outline how owning a home is beneficial in almost every statistical category. It would behoove you to read the whole thing. We will highlight some stuff here. But the point isn't to steroid your sales tactics. No, the point is to revolutionize your "why" so you can be all that you need to be in order to do all that you need to do.

We desperately need you to function at your capacity. Our country needs real estate agents who are outstanding at their job, who focus on all the right things and advocate for people in the right way. The result of your work benefits everyone. Your work enhances the safety and financial stability of each family and community. Our communities are significantly worse off without you, and we will prove it. We cannot overemphasize your value. It's impossible. Your role in our society is mission critical. Each day you are increasingly valuable, and my honest desire is for you to embrace your capacity and thrive. We all need you to do an incredible job. We are relying on you.

Owning a home isn't just good for the homeowner – it's good for the entire community. Homeowners are more likely to participate in local events, volunteer for community organizations, and invest in their neighborhoods. This creates a sense of community pride and fosters stability, which can lead to reduced crime rates and increased property values. As a real estate agent, you have the power to promote community stability and engagement by helping your clients find a home that they love in a community that they care about.

Here are some quotes and stats that we found fascinating. Most of these come directly from the NAR's 2016 paper. The rest are noted.

Friendship & Stability

"Homeowners are significantly more likely to make friends with their neighbors than renters are."

"Homeownership provides social benefits. Many sociology studies have found that residential stability strengthens social ties with neighbors."

People who own homes are more likely to be involved in their community and build relationships with other people in the community, providing them with a solid foundation upon which to build their lives.

Studies show that homeowners are 11% more likely to be educated in ongoing political and social news.

Homeowners are 46% less likely to experience substance abuse or domestic issues.

Education

A study done by the American Neighborhood Reinvestment Project found that *children of homeowners get higher reading and math scores on average and are 116% more likely to graduate from college.*

These same children are 59% more likely to own their own home within 10 years of departing your household.

"Consistent findings show that homeownership does make a significant positive impact on educational achievement."

Green and White (1997) found that homeowners have a significant effect on their children's success. The decision to stay in school by teenage students is higher for those raised by home-owning parents compared to those in renter households.

They also found that daughters of homeowners have a much lower incidence of teenage pregnancy.

Parenting

"Homeownership promotes parental engagement by giving parents more options for managing financial hardships and reducing the severity of financial hardships when they do occur, thereby reducing stress and disengagement from children."

"The results of the study suggest that children of selected homeowners are more likely to participate in organized activities and have less screen time when compared with renters."

Health Benefits[1]

Homeowners have higher self-rated health when compared to non-homeowners. This study also showed homeowners have higher perceived control over their lives and higher self-esteem and happiness rates than renters.

"Homeowners report higher self-esteem and happiness than renters. For example, homeowners are more likely to believe that they can do things as well as anyone else, and they report higher self-ratings on their physical health even after controlling for age and socioeconomic factors. In addition to being more satisfied with their own personal situation than renters, homeowners also enjoy better physical and psychological health."

Crime

Research on crime and homeownership shows that homeowners are far less likely to become crime victims.[1]

"Homeownership boosts the educational performance of children, induces higher participation in civic and volunteering activity, improves health care outcomes, lowers crime rates and lessens welfare dependency."

Wow! Just wow! How incredible are these stats? Which one stood out to you? What thought mattered the most to you? Now use this information to be more outwardly focused and more connected to your "why".

You aren't only selling real estate; you are selling lifestyle. You are selling the success of your friends and family. Everything you do in the business is for your customer's benefit. The moment you begin calculating your commission FIRST is the day your business starts to die.

Do you want your friends to experience less crime? Sell them a house.

Do you want your community to pay less in taxes? Sell them a house.

Do you want the next generation to be more educated, get better jobs, have higher incomes and buy houses for themselves? Sell their parents a house.

Do you want lower teen pregnancies? Sell them a house!

Listen, we aren't just trying to blow smoke. And we certainly aren't arguing that buying a house automatically solves all social ills. However, it can certainly help. Besides, the dedication required to get to a place where someone can even buy a home requires the development of several critical skills that emphatically influence the quality of people's lives.

We are for you. We are for you without reservation. We applaud you. We see you. We notice you. We appreciate you. We respect you. We value you. And we love you.

---

1 https://www.fortunebuilders.com/benefits-of-homeownership/

The financial blueprint for real estate agents has been laid before you. What you do with it is up to you.

Our encouragement to you is to think correctly and completely about the business you are in. First and foremost, you are indeed a business owner. Thinking like a business owner is the primary key to keeping more of your hard-earned money. This understanding will be the undercurrent of your success. It will guide your decision making and catapult you to be a force in your market.

Now let me ask you a few final questions. What would the natural result be if you read this entire book and did nothing differently? What would your life look like in three years? five years? 10 years? How close or far away would you be to your ideal future self? How furious would you be if you found yourself in the exact same position 10 years from now? What would it feel like to know you settled for less than you and your family deserve? What would it feel like to look your grown kids in the eyes knowing you didn't give your all? Really feel it. What would life be like if you never made a change?

Now...take a deep breath in.

Take a moment to envision your future self again. Take a moment to feel that great sense of pride flowing through your body. Feel the satisfaction of a job well done. Feel what it's like to accomplish all you set out to do. Consciously think about it. Ponder it. What does it feel like? What does it look like? What is the expression on your face? What is your posture like? Are you confident or are you timid? Are you resilient or do you shrink back? Do you get pushed around or do you have excellent boundaries? What does it feel like to be who you are supposed to be? What does it feel like to do everything that you're supposed to do? What does it feel like to look yourself in the mirror and know beyond a shadow of a doubt that you have given your all? Meditate on it. Dwell on it. Let nothing distract you. Every tool is at your disposal to radically transform your own life and legacy. Take advantage of them! Don't be shy! You've got this.

You are amazing.

Now go sell some fucking houses!

Key Questions:

1. Do you intimately know what you are selling?
2. What social benefit was most shocking to you?
3. How will you use this information to solidify your "why"?

Action Steps:

1. Stop reading this book and get back to work.

About the Authors

Nathan Ganz recruited Mike Ross to work in financial services as a part of his team. After just two years of working together, they decided to go venture into the world of business ownership.

The firm they previously worked for highly encouraged them to work with small to mid-sized business owners. It didn't take long for them to learn that business owners hate paying taxes. So, in a quest to free up cash flow for their services, the journey to learn all about taxes began. The idea was, if they could find the money and make their services free, who wouldn't want their help?

Since their tax strategies had a positive impact with their bigger clients, they became curious about how their tax strategies would work for smaller businesses. Their thought was simple: if these strategies work for people who have a lot of help, they wondered what the impact would be to independent contractors who might have never been exposed to this level of planning.

Thankfully, the results were massive. In fact, the average real estate agent who uses their creative strategies gets a 10% take-home raise, net of their fees. The bookkeeping department was born out of a need for accountability. Their real estate agent clients loved their tax ideas but had a difficult time executing. So naturally, they provided a creative solution.

Today Mike and Nathan have spoken to thousands of real estate agents and have clients from coast to coast. They get an unhealthy amount of joy seeing their clients succeed. They live for that "aha" moment when everything changes.

This book is the culmination of hundreds of classes over the last decade. Thousands of agents have heard them speak and have paved the way for this business and book to exist.

Mike and Nathan co-own NW Premier based out of Vancouver, WA. Their mission is to be the go-to, trusted, financial advocates for real estate agents.

Printed in the USA
CPSIA information can be obtained
at www.ICGtesting.com
LVHW020359030124
767934LV00006B/192

9 798989 528011